The Detectives of Shangani

The Mystery of the Lost Rubies

Nahida Esmail

PUBLISHED BY
Mkuki na Nyota Publishers Ltd
P. O. Box 4246
Dar es Salaam, Tanzania
www.mkukinanyota.com

ISBN 978-9987-08-292-6

Visit www.mkukinanyota.com to read more about and to purchase any of Mkuki na Nyota books. You will also find featured authors, interviews and news about other publisher/author events. Sign up for our e-newsletters for updates on new releases and other announcements.

Distributed worldwide outside Africa by African Books Collective.
www.africanbookscollective.com

contents

Acknowledgment

The Burt Award for African Literature recognises excellence in young adults fiction from African countries. It supports the writing and publication of high quality, culturally relevant books and ensures their distribution to schools and libraries to help develop young people's literacy skills and foster their love of reading. The Award is generously sponsored by a Canadian philanthropist, Bill Burt and is part of the ongoing literacy programmes of the Children's Book project of Tanzania and CODE, a Canadian NGO supporting development through education for over 50 years.

Foreword

Since 2008, the Children's Book Project for Tanzania (CBP) has been supporting novel writing and publishing in English with the aim of promoting the learning of English for the youth in upper primary and secondary schools. In a country like Tanzania where English is not widely used outside the classroom, concerted efforts need to be made to support its acquisition through intensive and extensive reading.

The Burt Award for African Literature is aimed at producing books which show the local situation, depicting familiar environments in order to arouse the interest and enthusiasm of the reader. Consequently, students can develop the habit of reading and enjoying interesting stories while improving their English skills and, ultimately their ability to learn other subjects taught in English. It is indeed the expectation of the project that the Burt Award for African Literature will be a catalyst for success in other subjects.

CBP wishes to thank the panel of judges for their dedication and integrity, and both CODE and Mr. Burt for broaching and supporting the project and all our stakeholders, including writers, publishers, librarians, teachers and students. It is their collective participation in various ways that has made the project a success.

Pili Dumea
Executive Secretary
Children's Book Project for Tanzania

To my dear daughters Hafsah and Humairaa

Adventure awaits you...

Chapter One
School Holidays

"What things always chase each other but never overtake one another?" Bakari asked Omari, shouting above the school bell, its high-pitched *Triiiiiiing* sound echoing though the alleyways of Stone Town. Loud laughter and noisy chatter followed the bell's chime as the children flowed out from the school gate filling the narrow streets. It was the last day of school and the beginning of a long holiday. The chatter was alive with shrieks, and squeals of excitement. Bakari and Omari had completed Form One and had done well in their exams. Form Two sounded terrifying for the fourteen year olds but that was a worry for another day. Bakari was in high spirits and did not wait for an answer but tagged Omari and shouted, "Race you to the sugarcane stand!"

They were out of breath as they reached the stand. "Two big mugs please," Bakari gasped to the vendor standing behind the juice machine, ready to take orders. The hot afternoon sun and the high humidity made them perspire. Usually they would rush home after school so they could freshen up for their afternoon *madrassah*. Today, however, they could take as long as they wanted to get home. The afternoon *madrassah*, where children learnt to read the Quran and Arabic, was closed for two weeks.

"Do you know the answer or not?" Bakari quizzed a distracted Omari who was more interested in watching the man fluidly squeeze the sugarcane flesh than answer Bakari's riddle. The vendor pushed two long sugarcanes through the machine, turning the wheel effortlessly, flexing his biceps. The cane was squeezed to a pulp, letting out juice into a standing jug at the other end of the machine. When the jug became full, he poured the juice into two mugs and added ice-cubes. "The answer *is* wheels of a car," Bakari said.

More students came to buy the sweet juice. The boys sat down and took their time to relish the drink.

"A long holiday, to chill on the beach, swim, snorkel, and eat plenty of *changu* fish," Omari said dreamily. He felt as though a burden had been taken off his shoulders. "Holidays make me feel like I could fly," he said, spreading out his arms as if he was about to take off. Bakari laughed at his friend's enthusiasm, he rubbed his lips as he took the last sip. Feeling refreshed, they continued down the winding alleys of the ancient Stone Town, a UNESCO heritage site, savouring their freedom.

Like the rest of the town the houses in the narrow passageways lined up closely facing each other. Outside every house was a cement bench. This is where the Zanzibaris sat anytime of the day to take a break from their chores and catch up with the neighbourhood gossip. At the bottom of some of the buildings were shops that sold sweets, clothes, *paan*, bread, soft drinks, *mandazi, vitumbua*, and many other things.

As they walked towards their homes, Mr. Barretto, the owner of one of the shops nearby called them, "Aha! I see two happy boys today." To celebrate their first day of school holidays he handed them a sweet and a Big-G, the chewing gum they liked. The boys thanked him. "You must join us for swimming Mr. Barretto," Omari suggested. "Join you? I will race you in swimming and will win too!" he teased. Mr. Barreto was a kind and friendly man. His silvery white hair, perfectly brushed back and thick square-framed glasses on his tanned skin revealed his Goan background. Only a handful of Goan families were left in Zanzibar having arrived from India in the late 18th Century. The small island still had a fusion of cultures left from the time of the Portuguese explorers to the Omani Sultanate, the Indian merchants to the Persians. These foreign settlers merged with the native Bantu populations.

The two friends were next-door neighbours in an area called Shangani and had grown up together. Bakari's bedroom window was only a metre away from Omari's. There were times they would stand near their windows and talk to each other. Days when it was raining, they would both stretch out their hands to see who could bear the beating of the rain for longer. The rain would pitter-patter loudly on the corrugated tin roofs and sound like music to the boys' ears. The water would cover the narrow paths and reach their ankles. The two boys would challenge each other to ride a bicycle in the constricted alley and see who could outdo the other before the deep water would throw them off balance. They would then go and sip a soda in Mr. Barretto's shop.

They were always on the lookout for an adventure. The year before a girl had gone missing and the local community had believed that she had been seized by a *jinn* while she was out playing during *Maghrib*. This is the time that the Zanzibaris believe the *jinn* come out to bother and pester humans. The boys had listened to the commotion outside the little girl's house and had made notes. Then they investigated and discovered that the little girl's brother had taken her to her aunt's house without informing the parents, where both of them had fallen asleep.

One of their favourite games to play in the narrow streets was hide and seek. All the children of Shangani gathered together to play, in the morning and at night. In the late afternoon, they often went to Forodhani Gardens where all the boys of the Stone Town gathered to jump off the edge into the azure Indian Ocean waters and swim. The boys tried to outdo each other in their jumps and dives. They ran from the side and somersaulted in the air, landing with huge splashes. A crowd often gathered to watch the boys' performance. If a jump was really outstanding, applause broke out. This encouraged the boys to keep competing until they received the loudest whistles and shouts of praise.

As the sky started turning a golden red, and the call for the evening prayer was heard, the children would stop playing and get ready to leave to go home or pray in the nearby mosques. Stone Town had numerous mosques and when the *adhaan* was called the echoes could be heard in every corner. The streets filled with men dressed in *kanzus*, loose white robes flowing from the neck to the ankles, and *kofias* to cover their heads. It was rare to see any man entering the mosque without this traditional dress.

After the prayer, many people headed home to their families to eat supper. Others went to the Forodhani Gardens to enjoy food from the many street sellers. With the light of their kerosene lanterns, they sold almost any food, from octopus and squid to Zanzibar Pizza and *mishkaki* with chips and the favourite Zanzibar Mix, which contained fried cassava strips, with *bajias* and potato balls, served with hot cassava soup and *mishkaki*.

Bakari and Omari went to the Garden to eat Zanzibar Mix. They washed it down with sugarcane juice, which was far more popular than any soft drink. The boys lazily headed back and stopped every now and then to greet friends or relatives. They sat outside Mr. Barretto's shop before going home, sipping away at Azam's new pomegranate soda. Bakari had a new riddle to challenge Omari with, he asked, "There was a green house. Inside the green house, there was a white house. Inside the white house, there was a red house. Inside the red house, there were many babies. What is it?" They asked Mr. Barretto the riddle and he shook his head. "I don't know the answer," he said. "It's too late at night for me to think. When you figure it out, you let me know," he joked.

Omari was more attentive this time to the riddle and it took him a few seconds to figure out the answer, "Watermelon!" he shouted with glee, happy that he had solved a new riddle so quickly. "Wait until I give you *my* riddle to solve!" he teased Bakari, "It will take you over a month!"

By the time they reached home, the sky had turned into a black carpet with twinkling stars and a glowing moon. Bakari laughed at Omari's boastful statement and replied, "It's a challenge for tomorrow then!"

Chapter Two

Bibi Fatuma

The next day, Bakari had just arrived home from a dip in the sea when his parents gave him good news. "Bibi Fatuma will be visiting us in two days time," Bakari's mother announced. "Hooray!" he jumped about, ecstatic. "This is a surprise!" He wondered why his grandmother had not informed them about her visit as she normally did, usually a whole month or two before arriving. Bakari was a good weaver and had learnt the skill from his mother. He wove mats and bags as a present for his Bibi Fatuma. Usually it took him over a month to complete one project. "Now I won't even be able to weave her something nice," he complained. He was however, overjoyed and brushed aside all his thoughts about why she had not informed them earlier. He only thought of how he was going to make a nice present in time.

"Ohhhhhhh!" he said, "This means my holiday is going to get even better!" He did a small twirl across the room bumping into Omari as he entered, making his parents laugh. His grandmother always stayed at her beach house and would invite Bakari and his family to spend time there, she called the house 'Bayt-el-Jameel', which meant beautiful house; it was a perfect name.

Bibi Fatuma allowed Bakari to invite any of his friends over if he wished. This time Omari would be coming a lot as his parents had travelled to Dar es Salaam for a week and he had prefered to stay in Zanzibar with his aunt.

Bakari called Bibi Fatuma his favourite grandmother although technically she was not his actual grandmother. When he would explain the relationship to Omari he started by saying, "Bibi Fatuma is my paternal granduncle's wife," Omari would just shake his head. It sounded too complicated to figure out. Bakari teased, "Yes Omari, and my paternal granduncle's wife's niece's daughter…" Omari chased Bakari before he could go on any further. "I don't want to know about your paternal granduncle's wife's niece's daughter!" Omari said, and they both burst out laughing.

Bakari loved to talk about his Bibi Fatuma, "Her father's great uncle was from the lineage of the first Arab ruler of Zanzibar, Sultan Seyyid Said, who ruled from 1804 to 1856 and made Zanzibar the seat of government in 1840." Omari knew this sentence by heart. He had heard it many times from Bakari. He mimed Bakari and they both ended up chuckling. Bakari's father, Musa, had told them, "Bibi Fatuma has some of the Sultan's characteristics. Just like him, she is tall in stature and her face expresses kindness and justice. Just like him, she is regarded as a model for justice." The boys had heard Bakari's father narrate the story of the Sultan many times. He told them about one of the Sultan's buildings which he called 'Bayt-el-Mtoni' or 'House of the Stream'. "It was a grand palace, one of the largest palaces built in Zanzibar during his reign, and housed more than a thousand people."

The day approached when Bibi Fatuma was to arrive. Bakari went with his father to make preparations that the required groceries and vegetables were delivered. Normally, since she usually announced her arrival at least a month before, the preparations were done slowly and leisurely but this time things had to move at a faster pace. She visited them at least once a year, sometimes even twice. The grandfather clock that was tucked in a corner of the room caught Bakari's father's attention as he noticed a film of dust on its face. "That clock needs to be wound," he said loudly to himself. It was his way of making a mental note as he was responsible for the maintenance of the clock.

On the day of his aunt's arrival, Bakari's parents went to pick her up from the airport by taxi. They couldn't get her normal driver at such short notice. They were however, equally excited to have her come and visit them. Bakari's father had given Bakari and Omari the task of overseeing the cleaning and finishing any last minute chores.

Bakari had been eager to go to the airport but also wanted his beloved Bibi to come home to a clean house. Her house, Bayt-el-Jameel, was huge and known as an Omani-style rest-house. It resembled the Sultan Seyyid's 'Bayt-el-Mtoni,' Bakari's father had told them about. While Bayt-el-Jameel was much smaller, it was nonetheless just as intricate. The house consisted of an audience chamber decorated with long mirrors; the floor was paved with marble slabs. Large pillars and archways were the main features on the windowless ground floor. The living quarters were based on the upper floor accessible from the audience chamber. It was a magnificent house although Bibi Fatuma had told them, "You should have seen this place in its days of glory. It was filled in splendour, nothing compared to how it is today." In the rear courtyard, there was a block of domed Persian baths that were still in use, unlike in other houses that had become ruins. There was a mosque built at the end of the house, for use by the family.

Bibi Fatuma had also maintained the garden very well. It was still lush, serene, and visited by many birds. Some of the archways in the garden were chipped, revealing the decades they had stood there. She had also let peacocks, ducks, fowls, and even a few gazelles occupy the gardens. There were three gardeners who maintained it while she was away. Bakari and Omari had completed the chores they had been given and everything was ready for Bibi Fatuma's arrival. They did a final round of the house checking on the maids and were satisfied that the work was done.

In the garden, Bakari jumped into the hammock placed under a tree. It made for a perfect afternoon nap. The rope that held it high had become loose and could not hold his weight. Plonk! The hammock fell to the ground, Bakari going with it! "Ouch! This hammock could have killed me," Bakari moaned in exaggeration. "Oh, poor hammock!" teased Omari, "I hope you didn't hurt it with your weight!" The boys laughed and Bakari chased Omari around the garden. Omari ran towards the tree house and stopped at the trunk. Bibi Fatuma had told the boys the story of the tree house. She said that the tree house at Bayt-el-Jameel was one of a kind in Zanzibar. This was because her father used to have many foreign visitors due to his business. On one occasion, an English gentleman had seen Bibi Fatuma playing with her dolls indoors and remarked that she with such a beautiful garden, she should be playing there instead. So he suggested her father build a playhouse in the branches of the biggest tree. "We should go and relax in the tree house later," he said, catching his breath. "Sounds like a good plan to me," replied Bakari, "After I catch you!" he said charging towards Omari. When the boys finished chasing each other they lay on the grass to recover.

Bakari admired the main door with its elaborate design and brass studs, which originated from India. When Bakari had asked Bibi Fatuma about the brass studs on the doors she had explained, "The Indians used these brass studs as a way to protect their houses and buildings from elephants."

Bakari had taken this information in as a surprise. "Wow!" he had responded, "Imagine elephants running around the alleyways of Zanzibar!" Bibi Fatuma also pointed out the intricate designs on the doors, "a door with a rounded top shows Indian design influence," she had explained. She further elaborated the reason for this Indian influence, "since many of the builders and craftsmen used in constructing Zanzibar were from the sub-continent, they brought their ideas with them."

Bakari and Omari petted the tame gazelles that wandered around the garden. They also looked through the astrological telescope that Bibi Fatuma used for viewing the stars and planets at night. In the past, they had spotted dolphins and a whale in the middle of the ocean using the telescope. The boys were allowed to use the telescope if they wished but they were always very careful whenever they did. It was very precious to Bibi Fatuma.

They climbed up the tree house and dusted the ground before they sat down. The branches had overgrown and needed to be pruned. "A perfect hideaway," winked Omari. They had once hid in it hoping they could play for longer and not have to go for their afternoon *madrassah*. They had many memories of the tree house. "Let's play a word scramble while we wait," Bakari suggested.

Bakari took out a folded piece of paper from his pocket and wrote down, *Lab Iotas*.

"Let me show you how to win Omari," he teased. This was a new game they had learnt at school and were also known as anagrams. They would scramble up letters and give them to the other with the goal of rearranging the letters into a word, sometimes giving a hint if the other was stuck. They were getting very good at the game and now would time each other to see how long the other would take to guess the answer. Bakari said, "I'm giving you a hint Omari, you can use this on water." Omari stared at the letters. He scrunched his eyebrows and within a few seconds, his frown broke into a smile. "Easy-peesy Bakari! You need to give me something more challenging!" He wrote down the answer, *sailboat*.

Then it was Omari's turn to write down a set of scrambled letters, he wrote, *Stereo Hue*.

"The clue for this is that you can climb up this thing."

Bakari looked at the scrambled words, thought about which letter the word could start with and suddenly came to an answer, "Tree house!" he laughed.

They stretched out their legs and enjoyed the view through the branches. From the tree house they could see some of the smaller islands. They knew the names of two – Snake Island and Changuu Island. They weren't sure if the other smaller ones had names. The sea appeared crystal clear, with many shades of green and turned blue where the sea met the African sky. They became mesmerised by the gentle swells of the waves, rising then dropping, creating foam as the waves crashed. The motion was hypnotising.

Hoot Hoot! A car horn sounded. The taxi driver alerted Bayt-el-Jameel of Bibi Fatuma's arrival. The boys raced to the front door to welcome Bibi Fatuma as she got out of the car beaming. This is how Bakari always remembered her. She always wore a smile. It was as if she had no worries in the world.

Bakari ran straight into her arms and gave her a big, warm hug. "*Karibu* Bibi," he said excitedly. Omari greeted her by kissing her hand out of respect. She patted him on his head and smiled. She let out a sigh. She had come home to her family and to her childhood memories of growing up in this magnificent house. Bakari looked forward to his holiday as Bibi Fatuma loved to spoil him.

Bibi Fatuma was a plump woman with greased, smooth skin that gave a shine of health. She wore long dresses that reached her ankles and sleeves that covered her arms, leaving only her hands exposed. She always liked to drape her head with a *khanga*. She made sure the proverb and symmetrical pattern of the *khanga* was to her liking. When she went with Bakari to Darajani last year to buy one for herself, she had taken a long time to choose before purchasing. The one she wore today read, *Tulia tulia utakalo utalipata,* meaning 'Just be cool, you'll get what you want'.

Bibi Fatuma had a thriving honey business in Oman, which was taken care of by the many workers she had. Because of the help, she was able to take the time off for a long holiday in her favourite destination.

Bakari loved being with her in her mansion. He felt he was blessed to have a lovely relative like Bibi Fatuma and Bayt-el-Jameel was a place he always looked forward to exploring. Although he spent many holidays there, he always discovered a new place, view, or ornament that he hadn't noticed before. However, he was quite sure that he knew everything well in the house by now. Or was there a possibility that he was going to find something new this holiday?

Chapter Three

Bakari's Present

When they entered Bayt-el-Jameel everyone saw a huge lunch-time meal which had been prepared for Bibi Fatuma and the family.

Bong! Bong! Bong! They heard the grandfather clock come to life as the maid wound the key to adjust the times. Bong! Bong! Bong! It was as if the clock was also welcoming Bibi Fatuma.

They all sat down and began helping themselves to the piping hot meal of chicken *biriyani*, fried banana with coconut, sweet potatoes, grilled fish with rice, and a variety of salad. A meal fit for a queen! On the table there was fresh juice, orange, pineapple, and guava. Dessert was a selection of fresh fruit. Bibi Fatuma went for the *shokishoki*, it was her favourite as it wasn't available in Muscat, the city where she lived in Oman. After lunch they sat outside on the veranda to sip some Omani *kahawa* that Bibi Fatuma had brought with her. Bakari didn't like it much, it was a bitter drink, flavoured with cardamom. He just watched his family savour the hot drink. He preferred freshly squeezed orange juice.

The family caught up on events and spoke about what had happened in their lives since they had last seen one another. They reminisced on the past and talked about the future. Every time their cups became empty, they would call the maid over for a refill. This continued until late afternoon, when Bibi Fatuma decided to hand out presents. She also had a secret present for Bakari. For this present, she had made arrangements for someone to buy it in Zanzibar and to deliver it on the day she arrived. She was going to keep that for last. She took out dates, Omani gowns, caps, dried fruits, and many more items. Bakari received an Omani style cap and a white robe to wear to the *masjid*. He received a packet of biscuits made with dates and a variety of nuts. The best present of all was a storybook about a young Omani boy who solved mysteries, "This is for my Detectives of Shangani," she said. He was ecstatic. He didn't realise though that the best present was yet to come. Omari also received a cap and a robe.

Musa, Bakari's father, received a small ceremonial curved dagger called a *Khanjar*. It was worn during formal occasions in Oman and often described as an important symbol of male elegance. He also got a brown Omani national dress outfit; it came up to the ankles with long sleeves, a matching turban and a cane called the *Assa*. Bakari stood up to try out some of his father's gifts, "Baba, this will look better on me I think," he teased. His father winked at Bakari and thanked Bibi Fatuma and said, "Bibi Fatuma, why all these presents with your situation?" Bibi Fatuma shushed him and smiled saying, "Let me enjoy my moment Musa. Good times don't always last."

Bakari and Omari exchanged glances. What a strange remark to make, Bakari thought. He saw a disturbed look on his father's face but wasn't sure. His father was now smiling at Bibi Fatuma's remark.

Bakari quickly became distracted by more presents, "Wow! I love seeing so many presents, all in one room!" he said joyfully.

Bakari's mother received a traditional Omani garb, a colourful and vibrant dress to be worn over trousers called *Sirwal* and a matching headscarf. She also got a fragrant perfume. However, her eyes nearly popped out of her head when Bibi Fatuma handed her a stunning gold necklace to go with the gown; a fancy intricate chandelier necklace, beautifully handcrafted by skilled Omani craftsmen. Her name had been engraved in Arabic on it, also cut from a gold sheet and centred on a gold chain. It was a dazzling piece of work. "This is absolutely lovely Bibi Fatuma!" she exclaimed.

The maids and gardeners all received gifts to take home and were grateful for receiving such generosity. They believed that Bibi Fatuma was still a queen, only a queen can be so big-hearted and charitable. One of the maids whispered to another, "She is our true Queen of Hearts."

After the gifts had been handed out, Bibi Fatuma announced that she was going to have a rest. "I'm so tired and jet-lagged," she said.

"Yes Bibi Fatuma, you better get some rest," agreed Bakari.

"We shall catch up later," she said as she climbed up the stairs. As Bibi Fatuma announced her siesta, everyone seemed to scurry off to a different corner of the house. Maybe they had all gone to take a rest too. Bakari and Omari did not follow the norm of afternoon naps that were a custom in Zanzibar. All the shops and offices closed down for the owners to have a nap during the hottest part of the day. Siesta time was a serious thing. The boys thought it better to go explore Bayt-el-Jameel. They decided to go up to the top floor of the house. After all, it was a house with many mysteries and stories of the past. Before they went up, they heard the sound of a bicycle bell at the front door. They rushed out to see who it was and saw a man wearing a white robe and a cap approaching them on a bicycle. He had a parrot sitting on his shoulder. He stood in front of the boys and asked, "Are you Bakari?"

Bakari replied in the affirmative.

"This is a present for you from your Bibi Fatuma, his name is Mzee Kasuku." the man continued pointing at the bird.

Bakari stared at him in wonder, "Wow! What an amazing present! Are you sure this is for me?" The man on the bicycle laughed, "Yes, it's for a boy called Bakari. Are you sure you are Bakari?"

Bakari nodded still staring at the African grey parrot which sat quietly on the man's shoulder. "*Habari yako?*" it said suddenly. Omari and Bakari burst out into laughter. A talking parrot! This was definitely the best present Bakari had received in his life. The man explained that Bibi Fatuma had called him a few months ago and asked him to train the parrot so that when she arrived, she could give the present to Bakari. He had taught it over a thousand words.

"You taught the parrot to talk?" Omari asked raising his eyebrows, "How do you teach a parrot so many words in a few months?" Bakari further inquired.

The man who seemed to be in no hurry to leave, got off his bike and put the parrot on Bakari's shoulder. He started to explain the method of training a parrot, "Since parrots speak without always understanding the words it is easy to teach them to mimic the sounds. The way I trained him was that I placed a mirror between myself and the parrot." The man spoke in an animated manner using several hand gestures. He continued, "Then from behind the mirror I said the words that I wanted the parrot to learn. The parrot seeing his own reflection in the mirror thought it was another parrot speaking and imitated all that I said from behind the mirror. See, it's that easy!" He smiled at the boys, happy to have shared his secret.

"See, it's that easy," mimicked the parrot. Bakari was nervous with the parrot on his shoulder and stood as if frozen. He was scared the parrot would peck at his head if he moved. The trainer moved the parrot to Bakari's head. The parrot's feet felt ticklish on his head and he started giggling. The man held Bakari's shoulders and squeezed them. "Loosen up Bakari," he said, "You'll get so used to the parrot that you will even forget he is on your shoulder." He moved the parrot to Bakari's shoulder again and gave him a packet of seeds, explaining what foods Mzee Kasuku liked. "Seeds, nuts, and fruits are his favourite," he said. He gave the tip of his finger to the parrot to bite on and patted his head with the other, "Be good now Mzee Kasuku," he told the parrot. With this he got back on his bicycle and waved goodbye. "*Kwaheri*" replied the parrot.

Bakari would have liked to rush up to his grandmother and give her a big hug, but he knew she would be resting so he decided to thank her immensely later.

They went to the garden and tested the parrot's vocabulary. "What is your name?" Bakari asked. "What is your name?" repeated the parrot, "Mzee Kasuku", it continued. Omari and Bakari were impressed that the parrot could answer their question. "What is your name?" the parrot repeated. "I am Bakari and this is Omari," replied Bakari. "How are you today Bakari and Omari?" Mzee Kasuku added. "Fine, thank you," answered Bakari and Omari. The boys were very impressed with Mzee Kasuku. He was definitely an intelligent parrot.

"Let's do something else," Omari suggested after a while.

"Like exploring the house," winked Bakari.

"Yes, maybe we can find some hidden treasure," Omari joked. "We can show Mzee Kasuku how to find treasure!" Bakari laughed. It was both Bakari and Omari's dream that one day they would find hidden treasure in the house. They had heard many stories of the previous rich occupants and how their palaces had been full of sparkling gems – emeralds, rubies, pearls, sapphires, and diamonds. They hoped they would find real treasure, buried deep in the earth, hidden away by the Sultans of Zanzibar. Bakari and Omari had at times drawn treasure maps for each other. The challenge was who could get to the imaginary treasure first!

They had once heard that the Sultan had invited a friend and given him the most expensive drink in the whole wide world. That was because the drink had contained a crushed mother of pearl – the most lavish of its kind. "What a waste!" Bakari had cried when he heard this story. He had asked his father about this and his father had laughed, "It sounds like your source had his stories mixed up. He must have meant to tell you about Cleopatra. The Queen of Egypt gave the most lavish dinner in history. She crushed one large pearl from a pair of earrings, dissolved it in the liquid, and then drank it down." Bakari and Omari had twitched up their faces as if they were drinking the crushed pearls, "I'm sure it didn't taste any good!" Bakari said.

Starting from the right-hand side of the house, they took the parrot and climbed the wooden stairways to the top floor. This was not the first time they had explored the house. They called themselves, 'The Detectives of Shangani', taking on the name Mr. Barretto had coined. "Maybe there's a mystery right under our noses," Bakari always said. Omari would finish off the sentence for him, "We have to just find it!"

The room opened onto a wooden balcony that overlooked a beautiful garden with many different trees, and past the garden was the Indian Ocean. The view was splendid. The door was an original Omani Arab style one, a simple traditional door with horizontal lintels. To the right of the door was an old fig tree.

They went into another room that looked similar to the first. It had a slightly different view from the balcony but was also magnificent. There was a small door that looked like a storeroom. Bakari and Omari had never been in there before as it had always been locked. They had both wondered what could be in there. Perhaps it stored a room full of treasures? They had been tempted to pick the padlock many times but thought it would be wrong to do so. Bakari walked up to the door and inspected the padlock. It looked old and rusty. To his surprise, he found that it was not bolted but just latched on. Bakari creased his eyebrows and whistled, "Too easy for Sherlock Holmes."

They removed the padlock and the door opened with a creek. It was dark inside. Omari took out his mobile phone and switched on the torch. It gave them just enough light to see the outlines of what was inside. They stood for a few moments staring into the room. The parrot suddenly whistled and they both jumped. The fright sent them into a fit of giggles. When their eyes adjusted to the dim light, they could see that the room was indeed a storeroom. There were many things piled on top of each other. Bags, books, rolls of material, and many more things they could not make out. In the corner nearest to the door, where there was more light, was a Zanzibar chest. Bakari nudged at Omari, "See, I told you, there's our chest full of diamonds and rubies!"

They decided to pull it out of the storeroom and take a look. Bakari knew Bibi Fatuma would not mind, she had never forbidden him from touching anything in the house, as long as he was careful. The chest was covered with a layer of dust. They found a cloth nearby and wiped the chest down. The design was beautiful. When they opened it, it was full of old rusty things. There was a book on top, full of dust, with torn pages and it seemed as though it had been eaten by moths.

"So this is your chest full of treasure," Omari laughed. Bakari's eyes rested on a clock with a red stone in the middle of the hands. He picked it up. He dusted it with the cloth. "There Omari, this is the treasure I was talking about, it looks like a ruby!"

"Good morning!" the parrot shouted suddenly. The clock fell from Bakari's hand as he got a shock. He had forgotten that the parrot was sitting on his shoulder. The glass smashed into pieces as it hit the ground. The red stone flew and landed near

the chest. Bakari and Omari looked at each other in fear. Bibi Fatuma might not be too happy if they had broken something important of hers. They decided they would show her the smashed clock and the stone that fell with it and explain what had happened. After all, they had not done it on purpose. They pushed the chest back into the small room and closed the door. Then they went downstairs and put the clock on a table. The two boys waited nervously for Bibi Fatuma to come out of her bedroom. Beads of sweat appeared on Bakari's forehead. He was thinking of how he would explain what had happened to Bibi Fatuma. He stood up, faced Omari, and started rehearsing what he was going to say to Bibi Fatuma.

"Bibi Fatuma, we were just looking at this clock and the parrot scared us." Omari raised his eyebrow, "That sounds stupid Bakari," he said.

"Okay, let me try again. Bibi Fatuma, here, we found a beautiful stone for you. But this clock, it got smashed. I hope it's not a precious clock or anything," he continued. Omari shook his head in disapproval.

"Okay Sherlock Holmes," Bakari said, sounding frustrated, "If you think you can say it better, then let's hear it." Omari started, "Bibi Fatuma, see, urm, see we were just, urmm, see, it was not our fault..."

"Please Omari, Stop!" Bakari interrupted. A look of worry passed over Omari's face. The boys kept quiet and silently rehearsed what they were going to say to Bibi Fatuma.

Chapter Four

Ruby Trail

Bong! Bong! Bong! They heard the grandfather's clock sound again as they sat in the family room that led to the lounge. Bibi Fatuma would be coming downstairs soon. They knew she enjoyed listening to the loud tick-tock of the clock and the loud bongs reminded her of the time when she lived in the huge house.

Click! They heard Bibi Fatuma close her bedroom door. They waited nervously until she was settled in the lounge. They followed her into the room, carrying the broken clock and the red stone in their hands. As they approached her, she looked up at them with a smile.

"Good evening boys," she chirped.

"Good evening Bibi," they replied. They stood there not knowing how to tell her. Bakari walked towards her and gave his Bibi Fatuma a big hug, thanking her for the parrot. "I love the parrot! Thank you so much!" Bibi Fatuma blushed. It gave her pleasure to see other people happy. "Well, I'm glad," she said.

"My name is Mzee Kasuku," the parrot decided to introduce himself.

"Well, well, Mzee Kasuku, nice to meet you," Bibi Fatuma said smiling, impressed by the bird.

"B-B-but there's a bit of bad news too," Bakari stammered. "How bad is it Bakari? You're stammering," Bibi Fatuma questioned. She knew Bakari well. He only stammered if he was very nervous. "I don't know Bibi Fatuma, but we broke something of yours," Bakari started, "by accident," he hurriedly added. Bibi Fatuma looked intently at them, wanting to know what they had broken. Omari pointed to the broken clock on the table and they both lowered their heads and said in chorus, "We're sorry, it was a mistake."

Bibi Fatuma took the clock in her hand and looked at it for a long time, she gestured to them to sit down. She did not look angry at all.

Her facial expression then changed and became more serious, "This clock belonged to my great grandfather and it was a gift from the Sultan himself," she said with a sigh. "He had helped the Sultan with something and in return he was gifted with this." Bakari stretched out his hand to show Bibi Fatuma the red stone that had fallen off the clock. Bibi Fatuma's eyes sparkled. "This is the ruby that my grandfather always spoke of. It's beautiful," she said, staring at it. Omari and Bakari looked at each other with a shocked expression. Had they really found treasure so easily? They didn't even have to follow a map or encode any secret letters!

As she stared at it longer, her face darkened. Then she shook her head. Bakari noticed that she looked sad. A few grey hairs peeped out of the *khanga* she wore to cover her head as her scarf. He read what was written on it, *Zawadi ni zawadi, usichoke kupokea*, meaning 'a gift is a gift, don't get tired of receiving'. She definitely did not tire of giving gifts, he thought. She was sitting upright but Bakari noticed a slight hunch in her back. Her face was full of tiny wrinkles. Bakari had never noticed these wrinkles on her face before. Where had they come from? Had they always been there? It didn't really matter to him because she still looked pretty to him.

She spoke slowly and softly, "This stone is..." and she stopped. She was searching for words to describe the ruby. "I wish I didn't believe this but this stone is the cause of many disasters," she managed to complete her sentence. "Maybe the reason for my existing problems is because of this very ruby," she continued but not clarifying what she meant. What existing problems? Bakari thought. Bakari creased his face. Long wrinkles appeared on his young face and he looked confused. He had never heard about this, a stone causing disaster in his family? How could that be? He saw that Bibi Fatuma looked sad so he didn't ask her any questions.

Omari and Bakari decided to leave her to her thoughts. As they quietly stepped out of the room, she called them back and said, "Bakari, I need you to take this stone and throw it away in the ocean. If my family hasn't benefitted from it in the past, I don't see how it can benefit us now!" She stretched out her hand holding the ruby in her palm. Bakari took the ruby. He looked shocked and his mouth fell open. He was surprised at the instruction. Throw away a ruby? A bright red ruby the size of a lemon! A real treasure that he had found in an old Zanzibari chest! How could he just throw it away into the ocean?

On top of that, it was a genuine ruby, a precious stone. He had written an assignment about rubies in school and he understood the stone's value. What a crazy thing to do! He decided that he was going to find out more about this stone before he did what he was asked to do. But he didn't tell Bibi Fatuma that. Instead he just hugged her and kissed her on her cheek before leaving the room. They decided that the first step was to go to his parents and ask them about the ruby. He was definitely not going to throw such a precious stone away without finding out the reason for Bibi Fatuma's strange decision.

His parents were at their home in Shangani. They were sitting on their veranda. His father was reading a newspaper and his mother was weaving a basket for a customer. His father's eyes nearly bulged out when he saw the stone. His mother let out a shriek of surprise! "Wow, Musa!" she blurted out, "Is this what I think it is?" "Where did you find this?" Bakari's father asked. Bakari and Omari retold the whole story. He stared at the ruby and his face looked thoughtful. He then gestured to the boys to sit down.

"Listen to the story of this ruby," he began. "This ruby belonged to your great, great grandfather who was a distant relative of the Sultan and also worked at the palace. He was a good man and the Sultan really liked him. This made many people jealous and so they plotted against him. The Sultan gave the ruby as a gift to him in return for a good deed your great, great grandfather had done for him. This only made people more jealous. They began to talk negatively about him to the Sultan and made up lies. Then one day, the Queen's pearl necklace went missing. The enemies plotted it in such a way that he would appear to have stolen it. However, the plan failed because the necklace was found. He continued being the Sultan's favourite and kept receiving precious stones as rewards for his dedication. Your great, great grandfather's favourite stones were rubies. It is thought that he had collected many, worth millions today. When he passed away, the rubies were not found and no one knows what happened to them. Many people believe that they are hidden away somewhere on this very island till today."

Bakari and Omari listened attentively. Rubies worth millions had gone missing! How was that possible? Bakari hadn't digested this new story fully but he had a string of questions. "What happened to him? How did he die? Was he killed? Did anyone try to find the rubies? Why haven't you ever mentioned this before?" he questioned his father.

Bakari's father let out a big sigh before he began to answer the questions. Bakari understood that there was something worrying him. Whenever his father sighed like this, it meant something was disturbing him.

"Bibi Fatuma feels that the rubies are bad luck," he explained. Bakari and Omari's mouths fell open. "What!" they both exclaimed at the same time. They had learnt in their *madrassa* that nothing can cause good or bad fortunes except God.

"How can that be Baba?" asked Bakari, "Do you believe that?"

Bakari's father shook his head saying, "Of course I don't! Only God can benefit or harm us, not a stone! But Bibi Fatuma has had many bad experiences and she has related them to a ruby she owned."

"What do you mean?" Bakari asked.

"Well," he said, not sure where to start. "I'll give you a small example. Before she owned the ruby, her health seemed fine but once the ruby came into her possession, she became very weak and feeble. She sold that ruby for a lot of money. As soon as she did, she felt her health return. That is just one example of many and that is why she doesn't want to keep any stones with her. She either sells them, gives them away or throws them away!" he explained. Bakari scratched his head; this was too confusing for him to understand.

"Can't we just explain to her that a stone can't cause bad or good luck? Her health could have just been a mental thing. She must have imagined that she got more sick," Bakari said trying to understand the situation.

"I wish it was that easy Bakari, especially now that her business is doing so badly," explained Bakari's father, "She even wants to sell her Bayt-el-Jameel and…" He stopped halfway through his sentence realising he had said too much. "What?!" they both shouted in chorus.

"What!" shouted Mzee Kasuku imitating the boys. He had jumped off Bakari's shoulder and was perched on a chair.

"She wants to sell Bayt-el-Jameel?!" Bakari asked not believing what he had heard. He had to repeat the words in his head for them to sink in. Bibi Fatuma's business had taken a bad turn and she wanted to sell her beautiful house that was full of memories? What had happened? Why hadn't anyone told him about this? Why hadn't he figured out that there was some problem? Could he do anything to help? If he could help in some way, then possibly Bibi Fatuma wouldn't have to sell Bayt-el-Jameel. He and Omari had to think of something!

Chapter Five

The Map

In order to distract themselves, they returned to Bayt-el-Jameel and went to gather the pieces of the broken clock. They hoped to stick the pieces together with superglue. It had great sentimental value to Bibi Fatuma. She had not been angry but the least they could do was to glue it together and put it back in the chest. They gathered all the broken pieces and started fixing it. As they were fixing the base, Omari noticed a small string hanging out which prevented the bottom cover to close properly. He had a small twig in his hand, so he used it to push the string back in the hole so the cover could close. The string however, wouldn't go back in. Omari decided to pull the string out and then superglue it back. As he started tugging the string, a long, slim sisal bag started to appear.

He elbowed Bakari. "Oh my gosh! What is this!" he shouted excitedly. They slowly opened the sisal bag and found a paper tightly rolled inside. It was as thin as the small twig they had used. It looked delicate so they had to be careful to roll it open. "Slowly," whispered Bakari. Omari wiped off the sweat that had formed on his brow and then rolled open the paper delicately. "Steady now." Bakari cautioned again, "It looks fragile." It appeared to be an old map. Bakari's eyes nearly popped out, "Do you think this is what I think it is Omari! Could this be real?" He was so excited his voice automatically turned into a whisper. They were intrigued. "It looks as though it has been in this clock for many years!" Bakari declared.

The edges of the map were rough. As Omari skilfully rolled up the map, one of the edges crumbled. "Oh no!" groaned Bakari, "We better be careful before the whole map crumbles".

"I have an idea," Omari suggested and he clicked his fingers. He took out his mobile phone from his pocket. "Let's save it," he said. Bakari looked confused at Omari's suggestion. Omari laughed, "Don't look shocked! Let's take a picture of the map so we have it saved on the phone's memory, in case the map really does crumble up!"

"Smart thinking," Bakari beamed at the idea. "Smart thinking," Mzee Kasuku said approvingly. "Why thank you, Mzee Kasuku," Omari said, taking a dramatic bow.

Click! The image of the map was saved on Omari's phone. They looked at the map, holding it at the edges to keep it from rolling shut. As they studied it, they noticed there was scribbling all over it in Roman and Arabic letters. There was also a big cross in black ink, a drawing that looked like some trees and other scribbles the boys couldn't figure out at first glance. There was no mistaking that it was a treasure map. "We should show this to Baba!" Bakari suggested. Omari nodded in agreement. He was still dazed at their discovery. They didn't want to get too excited about it before showing it to someone.

"Let's go now," Omari suggested as he jumped to his feet, "I'm sure he can tell us what this is about." "I don't believe how our day has turned out," Bakari speculated, "We find a real treasure and now we find what may be a treasure map!"

They placed the broken clock on a high mantelpiece, deciding that they would return to fix it. As they ran down the stairs, they heard a loud laughter. They could make out a deep voice of a man. As they entered the lounge, a man with a large build sat in a chair opposite Bibi Fatuma. As the boys greeted him, they couldn't help but notice a big scar on his right cheek that disappeared into a thick beard. The overhead light shone off the top of his balding head as his dark eyes followed the boys. They went to Bibi Fatuma and shook her hand out of respect. Bakari had put the map safely into the sisal bag and then in his back pocket.

"Bibi Fatuma, guess what..." Omari started, wanting to share with her their discovery. Bakari glared at Omari and cut him off, "Yes Bibi Fatuma, guess what, this parrot is amazing and can really talk!" Bakari interjected quickly.

"*Habari gani?*" Mzee Kasuku asked. Bakari then nudged Omari, he would explain to him later that they should never mention anything about their discovery in front of someone they didn't know, especially this strange man.

Bibi Fatuma introduced the man to them, "This is Sher Shah Khan. He is my accountant and helps to take care of my business in Oman." The boys smiled at him. The man spoke in a thick voice, "Hello boys, you can call me Captain Cook, if you like". He laughed when he finished his sentence. Mzee Kasuku was quick to greet Captain Cook, "Hello Captain Cook," he said. Captain Cook was amused and replied, "Hello lovely bird."

The boys observed Captain Cook, he was tall with a large build and with a stomach that was protruded from under his belt as he sat comfortably on the couch. He seemed to have a very unique style. As he drank his tea, the boys expected him to gulp it down but rather, he drank in a gentle manner, holding the cup as if it was something very fragile and he took small sips.

He saw the boys looking at him and he gave them a big smile. A gold tooth sparkled amongst other polished white teeth.

Bakari and Omari averted their gaze and politely excused themselves and went to look for Bakari's father. "What a friendly and well-mannered man," Omari commented as they left. Bakari had reserved feelings about him though and wasn't sure if he liked him. There was something about the man that bothered him but he couldn't quite say what it was.

"Omari, we have to be cautious who we tell about our discovery," Bakari said in a serious tone. Omari nodded in agreement. He had been eager to tell Bibi Fatuma and in his excitement forgot about Captain Cook. As they were leaving, the boys heard the loud laughter again in the background. Both boys were lost in thought but when the parrot imitated Captain Cook's laughter, "Hohoho! Hahaha!" they couldn't hold back their giggles. They rushed out of the house, not wanting to offend anyone with Mzee Kasuku's laugh.

Chapter Six

Captain Cook

The next day, when Bakari and Omari were going up to their tree house, they saw Captain Cook sitting in the garden, having tea and reading the newspaper. Captain Cook gestured for them to come and join him, "Sit my boys and join me for some tea." They politely refused the tea but sat with him. Captain Cook had shaved off his beard and looked different than he did the day before. He looked much younger. As they sat together, he told them stories of his travels. He had travelled the globe and had many interesting stories. Due to this, he had gained the nickname 'Captain Cook'.

He spoke six different languages and had also lived in many countries around the world including: India; Belgium; Switzerland; South Africa; Thailand; Burma; Sri Lanka; Kenya; and the United States of America. He told them that he had made a fortune with treasure hunts. "Wow!" the boys shouted in chorus. It was their dream to find a real treasure and here they sat with a man who had made a fortune out of finding treasures. Maybe they could learn a lot from Captain Cook. Perhaps he really was wise and that was why Bibi Fatuma had him as her financial advisor. Then he became serious, looked around suspiciously and asked, "Where can you always find money?" The boys thought that possibly he meant the treasures he had found but then he whispered the answer, "In the dictionary!" Captain Cook burst out laughing and continued until he had tears in his eyes.

He told them he had just come to Zanzibar from the deserts of Egypt, "The deserts have many secrets that I would like to discover. I am, after all, a traveller and an explorer. The sun was a killer. I stayed there for a whole month." He held his chin and said, "It's good to shave; it feels clean!" The boys were intrigued and impressed and exchanged glances, both wondering the same thing, could they share their discovery with him? Bakari wasn't sure yet if he could completely trust him. His father had taught him an important lesson in life and emphasised, "Always trust your instincts Bakari."

It was time for *Zuhr* and the boys decided to go to the *masjid* and look for Baba. They had still not been able to talk to him about the map they had found. They excused themselves and left. Bakari was deep in thought and didn't hear when Omari asked, "What's up Bakari? What are you thinking?"

"You know Omari, there's something that Captain Cook said that doesn't make sense to me," he started. Omari raised his eyebrows, he hadn't noticed anything odd in Captain Cook's stories. If anything, Omari had been inspired. They reached the mosque when the call for prayer was being called. "We'll talk later," Bakari said as he rushed to join the line of men in prayer.

When the prayer finished, they met one of Bakari's mother's friends, *Dada* Halima, who joined them as they walked. This didn't give them any time to talk about Captain Cook and their recent discovery. When they reached Bakari's house, *Dada* Halima sat with his parents and she didn't appear to be in a rush to leave. The boys didn't want to bring up the subject of the map in front of her either. "Let's go back to the tree house to look at the map again," suggested Omari. "Great idea," Bakari agreed.

They made their way back to Bayt-el-Jameel. There was no one in the garden. They climbed up the tree house and took out the map. As they were about to study it, they heard a voice, "Don't worry Henry. It'll soon be ours." It was Captain Cook's voice. He had come back into the garden. He didn't realise there was a tree house above him and he didn't know that Omari and Bakari were listening and peeking down. "If I find or know of anything else, I will let you know," the boys heard him say before hanging up. He looked around to see if anyone had heard his conversation and then walked towards the house. What a strange conversation! Why had Captain Cook looked nervous while on the phone?

"What did you want to tell me earlier Bakari, about Captain Cook? What was odd about his stories?" Omari asked. Bakari lowered his voice as he spoke, "He said he had come straight from the deserts of Egypt to Zanzibar." Omari nodded but still looked puzzled. "He had shaved this morning right?" Bakari asked. "Yes, right," responded Omari still unable to make the link between Captain Cook's travel to Egypt and shaving. Bakari looked at Omari and realised he didn't get it. "Didn't you notice?" Bakari asked. "Just tell me!" Omari said sounding restless. Bakari explained, "If Captain Cook had come from the deserts of Egypt then he should have had a tan at least. He still looked pale and had no tan. He shaved this morning and the skin of his chin was the same colour as his face. How can that be?"

Omari scratched his head, "That's true!" He couldn't believe he hadn't noticed that. "What does that mean though? Is he lying?" Omari asked. Bakari responded, "Something is not right about Captain Cook. We need to find out what".

Omari thought otherwise, "You're reading too much into this Bakari. Possibly he added some salt and pepper to spice up his adventure stories. He may have been exaggerating. Think about it, he is taking care of Bibi Fatuma's finances and she must have reason to trust him."

Bakari didn't buy Omari's logic. His gut feeling was that there was something fishy about Captain Cook. He had to trust his instincts.

Chapter Seven

Map Reading

Bakari removed the map from his back pocket and carefully rolled it open. The boys wanted to see if they could make any sense of it. The map was wrinkled. There was a blot right in the middle. "It looks as though whoever drew this map must have dropped some tea or coffee on it," Bakari remarked pointing at the spot. There was an X in the middle of the map and a dotted trail leading to what looked like a group of islands. It was marked, 'Land is son (RIP)'. There was a symbol in the corner, representing North, South, and West. There were a few numbers on the map 5, 40, 6, 30, and 39. Something was written in beautiful Arabic calligraphy but neither of the boys could make out what it said. They sat quietly, thinking about all the information on the map. "What do you think this would lead to?" Bakari asked breaking the silence. "Real treasure that could help Bibi Fatuma and her business!" Omari replied. "If we do really find the Sultan's treasure do you think she will want it? Since she has this belief that precious stones can cause bad luck?" Bakari queried. "Maybe we're getting carried away," Omari reasoned, "Let's show this map to your father and see what he has to say first. This could even be a prank someone planned years ago!"

They finally agreed to go back to Baba. There was no one at home except Baba as Bakari's mother and *Dada* Halima had gone to the market. Baba was sitting and reading a newspaper and greeted Bakari and Omari with a smile. Bakari took the map from his pocket gingerly. "We have something we need to show you Baba," Bakari said looking serious. "Look at what we found at the bottom of the clock that broke," he said as he showed his father the map.

His father stared. "Is this real?" he asked turning the map around. "Be careful Baba!" Bakari cautioned, "It *is* real and also delicate." The boys told him the whole story of their discovery again. "Well, I don't know boys. I don't know what this means. Or what it could lead to. Or whether it's genuine," he admitted. The boys' hearts sank. They had expected Baba to get excited about the map and tell them that they were going to find treasure where it was marked with a big X.

"Do you recognise any of the landmarks?" Bakari asked. Baba put on his glasses and studied the map. He did recognise many of the markings and tapped his finger on the map and on what looked like a group of islands. "These islands look familiar," he said, "Like the islands in the north-west of Stone Town," he added. He looked closely at the map then nodded. "Yes, this is Changuu Island, this is Chapwani Island, this is Snake Island, and this is Bawe Island," he confirmed pointing at each one. Baba had been a fisherman in his earlier years and knew the landmarks and islands very well. The islands were also visible from Bayt-el-Jameel and the boys could see them from the tree house. "What do you think 'Land is son

(RIP)' means?" Bakari questioned. "Well," Baba said scratching his head, "I'm not sure. But RIP stands for 'Rest in Peace', so maybe someone died there."

He turned the map around a few times to try to read what was written in the Arabic calligraphy. "Mmmm," he sighed, "This is beautifully written. The person who wrote this must have been very good at Arabic calligraphy. It is too small for me to see properly."

"A magnifying glass should do the job," suggested Omari. "Great idea!" Bakari agreed, "Just one thing, where can we find a magnifying glass?"

Omari scratched his head. Then he smiled. Any time an idea came to his mind, his smile would stretch all the way to both ears and his eyes would grow wide. He took out his mobile phone and searched through the pictures. He opened the picture of the map and zoomed in on the Arabic letters. He passed it on to Bakari's father who examined the enlarged image. He turned the mobile around a few times. His lips broke into a grin. "I know what this means," he finally said. Bakari and Omari were impatient. They were sure it must be a clue to the hidden treasure. It reads, '*Man Jadda Wajada*', which means, 'He who is serious, will be successful'," read Bakari's father. "*Man Jadda Wajada*," repeated Mzee Kasuku.

"What?!" the boys exclaimed.

"That sounds like a piece of advice and not a clue to anything. Perhaps this is not a treasure map, after all." Bakari said sounding disappointed. "Don't give up easily Bakari," Omari encouraged, "Maybe it is a clue to something. Let's analyse more of the map."

Bakari's father was a bit sceptical. He didn't think the map would really lead to anything, but he also didn't want to spoil the boys' fun. "Well, I hope the map leads somewhere boys. All the best!" he said, and then added, "You need to tell Bibi Fatuma about this map if you believe it is real."

"Yes Baba," Bakari said, "We were going to tell her earlier but she was with someone and we didn't get a chance."

"Okay," Baba replied, "Tell her when you can. Okay?" he said waiting for a reply. The boys nodded. "I have to go to work now. See you later!" Baba said as he got on his bike and rode off.

"See you later!" replied Mzee Kasuku who had left Bakari's shoulder to sit on the windowsill. "*Man Jadda Wajada, Man Jadda Wajada,*" Mzee Kasuku started singing on top of his voice. He must have liked the sound of the clue to want to turn it into a song.

Chapter Eight

Mr. Google

Omari widened his eyes as an idea came to his mind, "Maybe we should go and look through the chest again. Possibly we will find more clues," he said, sounding optimistic. "Come on, this is a real treasure hunt!"

"That does sound like an idea Omari. We can also search on the Internet and see if we can find any information." Bakari suggested catching on Omari's enthusiasm.

The boys decided to go to an Internet café around the corner to do some research. It was quite full and the boys had to wait a few minutes to get a computer. They were eager to surf the net for information. Bakari and Omari had fondly called the Google search engine 'Mr. Google', as they could always depend on it for help with their school assignments and general knowledge questions. They typed in the numbers that were written on the map, 5, 40, 6, 30 and 39, into the searchbar. Mzee Kasuku sat nearby, looking fascinated and listening to the typing sounds. Hearing the keys being punched so hard and fast he imitated the sound, "Click, click, click!" The boys turned to look at him and then continued with their research. There were a few results that came up. Bakari and Omari became excited; did this mean that these numbers would lead them to the treasure? Was it really a clue? Omari hit the result button and they read the following:

Zanzibar Geographical Position

The country of Zanzibar comprises the islands of Unguja (Zanzibar) and Pemba with the number of islets adjacent thereto. The island of Zanzibar is separated from the mainland of East Africa (Tanzania) by a channel which at its narrowest part is 36 km (22 1/2 miles) across. It lies between latitudes 5 40' and 6 30' South; and longitude 39 East. It is about 85 km (53 miles) in length and 39 km (24 miles)in breadth at its broadest point. Its area is about 1 660 square km (640 square miles). It is the largest island on the east coast of Africa

Bakari looked disappointed again and said, "These numbers show the geographical position on a map and that is all!" Omari reassured him, "Well, maybe it's a clue for something but we will realise it at a later stage. Let's search for more information and see what we can gather."

They then searched for the islands that Baba had mentioned. They read up on each island in detail and Bakari took down notes. He wrote in his notebook next to Grave Island, *A small section of it was used as a Christian cemetery since 1879.* They discovered that Snake Island was the very small island between Changuu and Chapwani islands. Boats do not usually land there as there is no beach. Bawe Island is an uninhabited island; many tourists go there for snorkelling. Changuu Island was also known as Kibandiko, Prison, or Quarantine Island. Large tortoises and peacocks are found on this island. Bakari scribbled all this information in his notebook.

There was a lot of information on Google. "We need to sit down and think about our clues again," Bakari suggested. Omari responded, "Let's go and look through the treasure chest again. We can always come back to the internet." Bakari agreed and they set off to Bayt-el-Jameel.

When they arrived back at the house, there was no one in sight. Bibi Fatuma had gone to the market with some of the maids. She would most probably return with Bakari's mother and spend the afternoon with her, or go visiting relatives and friends. Bibi Fatuma always had many people to see in Zanzibar.

The boys ran up the steps into the small room. They opened the lock and pulled out the chest so they could see better. They held their noses while opening it. It was still full of dust. Bakari took a handkerchief from his pocket and tied it around his nose and mouth. He started looking through the chest but the dust got into his eyes. Omari stood and watched Bakari. They didn't find much. Omari noticed an old dried up peacock feather and took it out, "I'll ask Bibi Fatuma if I can have this to use as a bookmark." They closed the lid and put it back. They looked at the broken clock that still needed to be glued together, maybe there were clues that they could still find in there. Bakari patted his pocket, the ruby was still there. He looked at the patterns on the clock and noticed that on either side of the clock was a very small drawing of a peacock. "Mmmm, someone must have liked peacocks," he said.

The boys sat on the bed and looked at their notes again. Bakari read out what he had written. Omari scratched his head. He started thinking aloud, "RIP, if these initials stand for 'Rest in Peace' and we know that Chapwani Island was known as Grave Island, maybe it indicates someone died there. Or that someone of significance was buried there. Changuu Island has peacocks on it. This clock has peacocks drawn on it. There seems to be no logical link. Snake and Bawe Islands are uninhabited". There really was no connection. The boys lay on the bed thinking. Bakari still looked in his notebook, then wrote down 'Land is son (RIP)'. He then wrote down all the names of the islands, the old and new. Snake, Bawe, Chapwani, Grave, Changuu, Kibandiko, Prison, and Quarantine.

Bakari looked up to see if Omari was following what he was doing but Omari was dozing with his mouth open. Mzee Kasuku had hopped on to the corner of the bed, and appeared to be snoozing also. Bakari smiled at the sight. He looked back down at his list and continued to see if he could find a pattern. Maybe there were similar letters or if he turned the names upside down, he would find something else. He tried to see if he could unscramble the sentence. When he started unscrambling, he could not believe what he came up with. He nudged Omari. Omari woke up with a start. "What happened?" he said still dazed from his nap.

Bakari pointed to his notebook to show Omari what he had unscrambled. Omari rubbed his eyes to wake himself up and see what Bakari had figured out. When scrambled, the letters from 'Land is son (RIP)' spelled Prison Island! Omari took the notebook to try out and see if Bakari had made a mistake. He hadn't! "Do you think the person who wrote 'Land is son (RIP)' on the map used it as a code to mean Prison Island?" Omari asked, his voice raising a pitch out of excitement. "Yes, it looks as though we've found a lead," said Bakari. "Let us go back and see if there is anything else Mr. Google can tell us on Prison Island," Omari suggested. Mzee Kasuku had also woken up with all the excitement and shouting from the boys. "*Habari gani?*" he said, indicating that he was awake. At first, Bakari was excited at having solved the scrambled words but then he appeared a bit doubtful. "Prison Island is a big island. Where will we start looking? We don't even know what we are looking for!" he said with hesitation. "Well, we don't know what we're looking for yet, but maybe when we get there, we will find a clue," Omari said, sounding thrilled and optimistic.

They returned to the Internet café which was now empty. Omari sat in front of the computer and typed *Prison Island* into the search bar to see what Google could come up with. "Wow!" shouted Bakari, "Look at how many results there are!" Google had found over a thousand results under that name. Omari pressed on the first result which read, *Changuu – Wikipedia, the free encyclopedia.* He clicked on it and they both read. "Well, Baba was right. Prison Island is now called Changuu Island. But it still doesn't give us a clue to anything," Omari said and went back to the list of results they had found. They next read, *Zanzibar: The Prison Island Tour.* He clicked on the link and as he skimmed through the material, a smile formed on his lips. His eyes became wider, Bakari was worried they will really pop out of their sockets. "So what idea do you have now Mr. Smarty Pants?" Bakari joked. "Bakari," Omari said enthusiastically, "Let's go on the Prison Island tour. Possibly we can find a clue while we are there." Bakari agreed with his friend, if it could lead them to any other clue, then that would be a good start. "Let's go!" Mzee Kasuku said, joining in their excitement.

Chapter Nine

Prison Island

The next morning they took a small boat from Forodhani in Stone Town across to Changuu Island. Bakari lowered Mzee Kasuku to his feet so he wouldn't fall off. The parrot wasn't happy with being put on the floor of the boat. He climbed back up onto Bakari's shoulder. Mzee Kasuku seemed to love the wind in his feathers and he stood upright as though to enjoy the wind more. He whistled loudly as if to say, What a lovely boat ride!

There were three visible islands from Stone Town and Changuu Island was the middle one. The waters were calm and it took them about twenty minutes to get there.

When they arrived at Changuu Island they had a good view of Stone Town. They could see the House of Wonders, known as Beit-el-Ajaib and the Old Fort clearly behind the Forodhani Gardens.

As the boys jumped off the boat, they felt the cool water on their feet. Both of them felt like going into the water for a swim but they knew it was important to investigate the island for a clue first. They could always come back to swim. They had decided to find a guide to take them around, even though they had read enough on the Internet. Perhaps the guide could tell them something that 'Mr. Google' couldn't.

The boys climbed up some stairs where they had to pay fees for visiting the island and joined a group of tourists. There were quite a few guides. One of them stepped forward and introduced himself as Charles. He had a medium build and small black curls on his head. He was a little cross-eyed which made it difficult to figure out who he was looking at when he spoke. He must have forgotten that he had just introduced himself as he did it again, "My name is Charles and I will be taking you around the island today."

Bakari and Omari exchanged glances and smiled. Charles asked for everyone to introduce themselves. When he was looking at someone, it appeared as if he was looking elsewhere. "I will be testing you along the way so you better listen to me," he joked. He then looked at Mzee Kasuku who was sitting quietly on Bakari's shoulder. "Before I start, let's see if you boys with the bird can answer this," he said smiling, "Why do birds fly south for the winter?" Bakari and Omari looked at each other. They weren't sure whether Charles was asking for a scientific explanation or whether he was joking. The tourists waited for someone to answer. Charles decided to answer himself. "Because it's too far to walk!" he chuckled. Mzee Kasuku imitated his laugh and that made everyone laugh.

"Let us see if any of you know what *Changuu* means?" he asked. Bakari and Omari raised their hands up to make sure Charles noticed them. They felt if he looked towards them they wouldn't know who he would pick on. Charles nodded towards Bakari to give the answer. Bakari looked to his left, where one of the eyes was pointing and then back at Charles, and asked, "Me?" Charles nodded and Bakari answered, "*Changu* is a name of a fish in Swahili and it is common in the seas around here." Charles grinned, "Clever," he complimented.

Charles took them around the island giving them historical facts along the way: "The island was once used by an Arab slave trader to contain troublesome slave. He had brought the slaves from the mainland and dumped them on the island to prevent them from escaping. In 1893, after the abolition of slavery, the island was inhabited by a British General, Lloyd Mathews, and under the orders of the British administrators a prison was built. The idea behind the prison was to send violent criminals from the Tanganyika mainland there," he said

They stood facing the old prison's crumbling cells, when one of the tourists asked, "Was it ever used as a prison?" Charles beamed; he loved it when the tourists were keen for more information. "Good question. No, the prison was never used to house prisoners, as was the original intention of the architects," he answered. "It ended up being used as a quarantine centre, instead of a prison, for yellow fever epidemics, especially during the outbreak of contagious diseases in the last century," he added.

Bakari and Omari had learned all this on Google. They were following their group but their minds were occupied with looking for clues to the treasure map. They were going to ask Charles about it at the end of the tour.

One of the tourists asked, "Why are there no wooden carved doors on this island like those seen on the mainland or in Stone Town?" Charles happily answered, "That's another very good question. As a matter of fact, there was a carved door that the Arab owner had put in the building, but a few years ago the door was broken down by some bandits. It was repaired and later taken to the museum and it is still there."

As they strolled through the forested interior, the boys recognised some of the indigenous trees: Indian Almond; Papaya; Citrus; and Frangipani. They spotted a variety of birds including colourful peacocks, and beautiful butterflies. One of the male peacocks spread its feathers, displaying the vibrant colours of its plumage. "Wow," gasped one of the tourists at the sight. "Breath-taking," another remarked. The boys were also captivated to see the peacock in its full glory.

The stroll did not take very long considering the size of the island; it was approximately 810m long and 230m wide, a fact they had learnt from Mr. Google. When they had returned to where they started, the group stopped to look at the tortoises. Charles explained about the conservation project that the island ran to preserve the Aldabra Giant tortoises. "Do you know where these tortoises are from?" Charles tested his audience. There were many guesses. "The Seychelles!" Omari shouted. "Well done!" Charles said winking at him. Although Omari wasn't sure if the wink was for him, as Charles's other eye was looking at the tourists. "Yes," continued Charles, "They were imported from the Seychelles in the late 19th century. This endangered species was a gift from the Government of the Seychelles." Changuu island is now more commonly known as the home of Zanzibar's Giant Aldabran Tortoise colony, some of which are over a hundred years old!"

When the tour concluded, and the tourists had asked their questions, the rest of the group decided to go snorkelling in the turquoise waters or sit on the white sands to bake in the sun. Bakari and Omari went to speak with Charles. "Ahh the smart boys," he said smiling as they approached him. "We wanted to ask you something," began Bakari. He looked at Charles' forehead when he talked, instead of his eyes, because he found it distracting when he thought Charles was looking somewhere else. "Oh, the smart boys don't know something!" he joked.

As Omari started explaining, Charles interrupted him, "Let me ask you clever boys and your clever parrot something," he laughed as he asked, "What do you get if you cross a cat with a parrot?" The boys looked at each other. They knew by now that Charles was asking them a riddle. Charles continued, "You clever boys don't know? Ok, let me give you another hint, what's orange and sounds like a parrot?" "A carrot!" answered Omari, proud at having solved the riddle. Mzee Kasuku repeated what Omari had said, "A carrot." Charles raised his eyebrows, "Clever boys and a clever parrot." He was going to ask them another riddle when Omari decided to interrupt him. "We wanted to ask you about an Arabic saying. He took out a paper where they had asked Baba to write the saying down: *Man Jadda Wajada*, 'He who is serious, will be successful', and showed it to Charles. His cross-eyes made him squint when reading and he had to bring the paper close to his face to read it properly. "Can you tell us anything about this saying," Omari asked. Charles recognised the saying at once and laughed. "Are you boys testing me?" he retorted. The boys looked confused. They didn't know what Charles meant. "The Zanzibar door that we were talking about earlier, the one which I mentioned has been moved to the museum, had this saying carved on it," he said laughing. "It is the only door in Zanzibar with this saying. Most of the other doors on the mainland have verses from the Qur'an engraved on them.

Are you sure you're not just testing me?" he asked again with his squinted eyes. The boys weren't sure which one of them he was looking at.

Both Bakari and Omari's mouths fell open at this information, they couldn't believe that there was a link to the saying they had found on the treasure map to a door that was on Prison Island. "Wow!" Bakari nearly shouted. Omari had to calm him down. "Perhaps the door is the lead to the treasure," Bakari said still excited. Omari had to tell him to speak softly. With the questions done from the boys, Charles decided to ask them another riddle.

"Knock, knock!" Charles said.

"Who's there?" Omari responded.

"Leaf." Charles continued.

"Leaf who?" Bakari responded.

"Leaf me alone!" Charles said as he burst out in laughter.

"Leave me alone," Mzee Kasuku repeated. This made the boys collapse into giggles.

They decided to return and as they got on the boat, Charles shouted, "Teach your parrot the number one rule for safety," and he paused. "Tell him not to fall off the boat!" he cracked up at his own joke. They thanked Charles and set off to the museum to inspect the door. They had come to Prison Island not knowing what clues they might find or whether there would be any clues at all. They were pleasantly surprised at having found such a strong lead to their treasure map, and felt they were definitely emulating the Arabic saying, they were striving and hoping for success.

Chapter Ten

The Museum and the Zanzibar Door

Omari and Bakari entered Beit-al-Amaan, 'Peace Memorial Museum', a remarkable structure designed by a British architect. The two boys appeared to be the only visitors. They paid the entrance fees and walked around the museum. To their dismay, there was not much to see. They walked to the receptionist and asked her where the Zanzibar doors were displayed. She shook her head, raised her eyebrows and shrugged her shoulders as a sign to say she didn't know. It looked like she had dozed off and they had disturbed her sleep. "What sort of a museum is this?" Bakari wondered. "You don't have anything in here. It's nearly empty." The woman shrugged her shoulders again. She didn't look the bit least concerned.

"We're wasting our time here," Bakari said. "We'd better leave." "I agree, let's leave, it seems as though this place is dead and the receptionist can't even bother to talk!" Omari said sounding annoyed at the receptionist's behaviour. Mzee Kasuku wasn't impressed with the woman's behaviour either, so he decided to sort her out. "Wake up! Wake up!" he started screaming. The woman looked alarmed. "Wake up! Wake up! Thief! Thief!" he screamed. The woman panicked. She looked around to see if there was anyone who had sneaked into the museum. Bakari and Omari found it hilarious and rushed out of the museum before Mzee Kasuku could make more trouble. "What was the woman worried about anyway, even if a thief had entered there, there was nothing to steal," Omari said as they walked out of the museum into the garden. A path led them to the back of the museum where there was a small building. It was an extension of the museum. "Maybe it's in this section?" Omari thought aloud.

As they entered, they were asked to pay again. Omari asked the man at the entrance, "We've come to see the Old Zanzibar doors." The man looked at Omari as if he had said something absurd. "Little boy," he said, "As you can see, this part of the museum keeps stuffed animals and there are photographs of the animals and insects found on the island. You've obviously come to the wrong place." Bakari and Omari felt angry with the man, but didn't say anything. They were not going to pay an entrance fee to go and see a photo exhibition when they were looking for a Zanzibari door! How could this museum be so empty, only having insects and animals of Zanzibar on display instead of all the antiques. "Does this mean that we don't have a clue to follow?" Bakari said in a low voice. "How can a big door just disappear?" Omari questioned. The man didn't answer their questions. He was unhelpful and rude. "If you have money to pay, you can go inside, if you don't you better beat it," he scoffed.

The boys turned around to walk out. Maybe they had been too excited about the lead. Maybe the map really meant nothing. As they were leaving the museum, they met a man coming towards them. The boys recognised him from Prison Island. He was the other guide named Rajabu, a friend of

Charles. The guides all returned to the mainland in the evening. None of them slept on Prison Island. The boys greeted him and asked if he knew anything about the Zanzibar door which Charles had told them about. "That door was kept right here in this museum, along with a lot of other antiques. However a few years ago, the museum was burgled, everything was taken!" The boys' mouths fell open! What! How could someone enter a museum and steal everything from it! "You mean the door was also stolen?" Omari asked, his heart sinking. Rajabu smiled, "Well, the door wasn't stolen, but after the burglary they decided to move the remaining items into the House of Wonders which has also been converted into a museum," he said.

The boys felt relieved. At least their clue was safe. "Well they should close this museum down. Not only is it empty, but the people working here don't seem to care much about anything," Bakari complained to Rajabu. Rajabu nodded sadly in agreement, "Yes, they should." With that, Omari and Bakari thanked Rajabu and hurried towards the bus station.

"Let's catch a *daladala* to the House of Wonders," suggested Bakari. Omari agreed. They got on a *daladala* with a sign that read, 'Mizingani Road'. They knew that was the road the House of Wonders was located on. Bakari paid the ticket fare and said, "Beit-el-Ajaib" which was the Arabic name for House of Wonders. The *daladala* stopped right outside the Beit-el-Ajaib which was on the town's seafront, facing the Forodhani Gardens. It was the largest and tallest building of Stone Town. It was situated between the Old Fort and the former Sultan's Palace, a building that had also been converted into a Museum. They had studied the building's history in school. It was named

'House of Wonders' because it was the first building in Zanzibar to have electricity, and the first building in East Africa to have an elevator. It was one of six palaces built by Barghash bin Said, the second Sultan of Zanzibar. As they entered the House of Wonders, a sign read, *The House of Wonders Museum of History & Culture of Zanzibar & the Swahili Coast.*

They had been at the House of Wonders many times, visiting with their parents, school, and friends. It was a magnificent structure. It was a four-storey building with a highly visible clock tower. There were beautiful white columns supporting the spacious verandas. At the centre was a large roofed courtyard surrounded by open galleries.

The boys would normally marvel at the enormous structure but today they were there for a purpose; they had to find the carved doors. They walked up to the first floor, taking wide strides on the large wooden staircase that wound up along the inner walls. The receptionist had told them that the first floor had the carved doors on display.

In the past, each floor had four giant carved wooden doors. The main door however had been removed and put on display on the first floor. Despite their size, there had been many incidents of huge doors being stolen and smuggled to different countries.

They stopped when they saw the doors on display on the first floor. The first door was the main door of the House of Wonders. It was covered with striking golden Arabic calligraphy inscriptions from the Qur'an. The door was wider than the other doors. Bakari and Omari had been taught that Sultan Barghash had wanted the main door to be wide enough so that he could easily ride an elephant through! They couldn't remember whether he had actually done that or not!

They asked the attendant of the first floor to show them the door that had been brought from Prison Island. He pointed them towards the door and followed them slowly. The boys looked at the door intensely. They could not really make out anything on it that looked different from the other doors. The calligraphy at the top was difficult for them to read and the motifs looked the same as all the other doors, pineapple, frankincense, beads, rosette flowers, and date palms. The attendant seemed eager to help. "What are you looking for boys?" he inquired. "We're looking for the door that was originally on the Prison Island with the inscription, 'Man Jadda Wajada', 'He who is serious, will be successful'", Bakari explained. The man slowly reached for something in his pocket. It was a retractable pocketsize measuring tape. He opened it a little to use it like a ruler to point to the Arabic writing on top of the door. He read it for them, "*Man Jadda Wajada*! Yes, this is the only door to have these words on it," he clarified. Bakari asked, "Is there anything else different on this door?" He smiled as he had had no one to talk to that morning, so he was glad the boys were enthusiastic.

He decided to give them a lesson on the doors. However, he took a painfully long time to explain things. He pointed with his measuring tape, turned pointing stick, to a board that explained what each symbol meant on the doors.

The symbols on Zanzibari doors

Flowers: *A flower represents a family; every flower that is found at the top of a door indicates that a distinct family lived inside. Often they were distant or close relatives, but were always distinct families.*

Pineapples: *Pineapples were a sign of welcome - similar to writing 'karibu' on a business sign.*

Fish scales: *Fish were caught for export to the mainland and even as far as Oman. This motif said that the owner was a fisherman - or traded fish.*

Rope: *This was commonly seen to symbolise security and also showed that the occupant owned fishing vessels.*

Chains: *it was a clear indication that the owner both possessed and traded slaves.*

Vines: *The owner dealt in the spice trade. Floral vines were appropriate symbols as pepper, vanilla and other spices often grow this way.*

Geometric squares: *Geometric designs indicated that the owner was a proficient mathematician and offered his services as an accountant.*

Beads: *The owner was a jeweller and specialised in precious stones.*

Arabic script: *The symbolic designs and quotations from the Koran were intended to exert a protective influence.*

Waves: *Waves of the sea climbing up the doorpost represented the livelihood of the Arab merchant to whom the house belonged.*

Frankincense and date palms: *These symbolised wealth.*

He then pointed with his ruler to the door that had been on Prison Island, "See this door has most of the symbols but it has one more thing that none of the other doors have." Bakari and Omari raised their eyebrows. The attendant pointed to a symbol which neither of the boys could make out immediately, "These are peacocks," he said. "Maybe they were carved because there are peacocks found on the island," he said, "But no one really knows the reason behind it". There were two peacocks carved on the door; one on either side. "Peacocks are not on the list of symbols on the board as these are an exception to this one door," he explained. By this time, the boys had decided to sit on the floor; they knew the explanation would take long. The man spoke slowly pronouncing each word clearly. Perhaps he wanted to ensure that the boys didn't miss any information. Bakari had his notebook out and was writing as the attendant spoke. He was rather happy with the attendant's slow pace as it gave him enough time to write everything down.

The attendant adjusted his glasses as he explained further, he began speaking slowly and taking his time, "However, there are some other places where similar peacocks like these are drawn." The boys sat up straight – paying full attention. They waited for him to tell them more. This information could definitely be another lead. He was scratching his head as if thinking how best to tell them. Then he abruptly said, "Follow me". He walked down the large wooden steps and out of the building. He walked at a fast pace, the complete opposite to how he spoke. He stopped to tell the receptionist something and continued to walk out. The boys had to skip a little to keep up with his pace. They followed him inquisitively; they had no idea where he was marching to.

The attendant crossed the road to the Forodhani Gardens. He then turned around to look at the House of Wonders from across the road, "Look there," he said, pointing at the large clock tower. Their gaze followed his fingertips, "Look at the side of the clock," he said. The boys could not see very clearly what the drawing was of, as it was rather small. Omari had an idea and he clicked his fingers. He took out his phone and put it on camera mode. Then he zoomed in on the image next to the clock. Click. He took a picture. He zoomed in further and they could see the drawing of a peacock. Just like on the door, one on either side of the clock. "This drawing of the peacocks is like the drawing on the small clock that we broke," Bakari whispered to Omari. The attendant looked pleased with himself. He was happy to have taught the boys something they did not know. After all, that was his job. They followed him back into the House of Wonders. Bakari had suggested they take a photo of the door and the carvings of the peacocks, so they can have a closer look again at home if they wished. "You can visit the Archives if you like," he suggested. "You can find more information on the door and the saying there," he added. "My friend Babu works there. I'm sure he'd be glad to help you out."

The boys thanked him and took a picture of the door. Omari pointed at the arch of the door as he realised Mzee Kasuku had quietly walked his way up. "He's posing for a photo!" Bakari chuckled. "Maybe he thinks the picture will look better with him in it!" Omari laughed as he clicked another picture for his new model. "Thank you!" shouted Mzee Kasuku as he made his way back on Bakari's shoulder. As they left the House of Wonders, they were both contemplating this new information; what did all these clues mean? Were the clues a link to the treasure map? What did the peacocks have to do with the treasure? Was the treasure possibly buried somewhere on Prison Island? What was the peacock drawing on the clock tower a sign of? Was the drawing of the peacocks on the small clock that they had broken linked to the peacocks on the clock tower of the House of Wonders? Did the clocks imply the importance of time? All the clues seemed separate. They had to figure out what the link was.

Chapter Eleven

Archives and the Zanzibar Door

"What time is it?" Bakari asked. "It's quarter past two," replied Omari, looking quizzically at Bakari. "We still have time to get to the Archives. Do you think we can make it if we ride on our bicycles?" asked Bakari. "Sure we can!" responded Omari enthusiastically, "Let's go find whatever information we can get about that saying," he insisted. They were not far from home, so they went quickly to get their bikes and cycled to the Archives.

They had learnt about the Zanzibar Archives at school, and they knew that the Archives kept a collection of original historical records and documents which provided a record of the past.

Bakari placed Mzee Kasuku into a customised wire basket on the front of the bicycle to keep him safe. Mzee Kasuku held onto the wires tightly with his claws and beak. He didn't want to fall off when the bicycle bumped into a pothole! The Archives were situated just outside the main town in an area called Kilimani. It was quite a distance from their house but the boys liked a challenge. They rode along Nyerere Road up to where the Mnazi Mmoja hospital was situated. They had to turn left off Nyerere Road and then take the first road on the right to get to the Archives. "Finally!" Bakari said a little bit out or breathe. "Finally!" repeated Mzee Kasuku out of relief as he hopped onto Bakari's shoulder. "Let's hope we find what we're looking for," Omari said. They left their bikes near the staircase and climbed to the first floor.

A sign outside the door read, "No food or pets allowed!" Bakari left Mzee Kasuku on the porch, hoping he would be safe there. As they opened the door, an attendant jumped from his seat to welcome them. "H-h-hello b-b-boys, h-how c-c-can I help you," he said with a stutter. He was short and plump with a fixed smile on his face. "Are you Babu?" Omari asked. "Yes," he nodded. "We're looking for any information you might have on the Zanzibar door that was found on the Prison Island with the saying, '*Man Jadda Wajada*' and the peacock design that it has on the side." Bakari blurted out, taking a deep breath at the last word.

"Ahhh," Babu said, a smile still fixed on his face. The boys' faces lit up at his response. Perhaps this eager archive attendant would solve the mystery for them, they thought. How wonderful that would be! He led them to the end of the room and gestured for them to sit down. The boys had to dust off their chairs before they sat down, it seemed like the Archives did not get many visitors. The shelf in front of them had many files that looked old, overflowing, and dirty.

Babu looked through the folders and returned holding a handful of heavy files. He appeared efficient and seemed to know where everything in the Archives was. He had hardly taken five minutes to retrieve the required files. As he laid the files on the table, dust flew from all the directions. "V-v-very old," Babu said, as if explaining the reason for the dust. He then sat down, pushed back his glasses and started turning the old, mouldy pages carefully.

The boys sat there patiently. Then he looked up at them and passed a file for them to look through. The boys also turned the pages slowly. The manuscripts were in Arabic and at the top of the file it was written, 17th century. From school, they knew that this was the time when the Omani sultans had taken control of Zanzibar. There were other things in the file including: stamps; newspapers; maps; and photos. All looked antique. They couldn't make out much in the file, so they looked through another. The other file was labelled 18th century and the other 19th century. The boys turned the pages of the file carefully.

The attendant pulled something from the file he was holding and gestured for the boys to come over to him. He pointed to a picture of the Zanzibar door that they had seen at the museum. It was a black and white photo. There was a lot of scribbling along the side of the photo but it was in Arabic. The boys could read and write Arabic but not when the writing was scrawled. They remembered from school that all Swahili literature was written in the Arabic script in the 18th century. It was only from the 19th century that the Latin script for writing the Swahili language was introduced.

Babu had also found a newspaper article and some other black and white photos of the door. Some pictures were a close up image of the symbols carved on the door. "Is there anything that explains what is written at the top of the door?" Omari asked. Babu pushed his glasses back further on his nose and flipped open the file once more. There was a poem titled '*Man Jadda Wajada*' and Babu pointed to it. "Can you please read it for us?" Bakari requested. Babu was more than delighted to be of help. He cleared his throat and read. It was written in Arabic script but the wording was in Kiswahili:

He who tries hard will find his reward
Strive – to get an award
Believe that you can
and Say "I can"
Strive and thrive to survive
Let this be your drive
Choose success
And with it you can impress
Humans are born to succeed
With hard work, success is guaranteed.
He who is serious, will be successful
Be serious – be useful
Strive while you are alive
You only have this one life
Success will come to you
All you have to do.........
...Is to try hard
And be on guard
...Is to try your best
For the test
And leave to destiny the rest
...Is to believe you can
Say "I can"

If you have the will
Only then will you climb the hill
Believe that you can
and Say "I can"

Bakari scribbled the poem in his notebook as Babu read it. Strangely enough, he had read the poem without a stutter. They asked him to read it twice more. "Wow!" Omari exclaimed. "What a beautiful message that is!" Bakari agreed, "It is a message of how to live your life."

Babu smiled at the boys. "I-I-I'm glad you liked the poem," he said, with the stutter returning. "Y-y-yes. If y-y-you want to s-s-succeed in life, y-y-you have to t-t-try v-v-very hard," he finished. The boys found it strange that he had been able to read the poem without a single stutter. They asked him if they could get a photocopy of the poem. "I'm sorry boys but the photocopier is not working today," he apologised. Bakari had written the poem down as Babu had read it, but they wanted it in its original form to put together with their other clues for later when they would look at everything or in case they needed to show the original to Baba. Then Omari had an idea and requested to take a picture of the original poem with his phone. "S-s-sure you can," Babu agreed smiling.

Chapter Twelve

The Clues

The boys decided to print the photos they had taken with Omari's phone so that everything could be laid out in front of them. There was a photocopy shop near Mr. Barretto's shop. They passed by to greet him. "What are the Detectives of Shangani so busy with these days?" he inquired. Bakari smiled and said, "We'll tell you when we've solved the mystery Mr. Barretto!" Omari winked at him. When the photos had been printed, they cycled to Bayt-el-Jameel. They climbed up the tree house and arranged all the papers: the treasure map; the Zanzibar door with the saying 'Man Jaddah Wajjada'; the peacock symbols on the door; the peacock drawings near the clock tower on the House of Wonders; and the poem. They had also brought the small clock from which they had found the treasure map and the ruby.

The boys looked at everything intently. They studied the photos quietly, each trying to figure out the meaning. "Well, we still don't know if this is really leading to anything," Bakari said scratching his head. They looked at the map again; specifically the dotted trail which led to Prison Island. They had been to Prison Island and found out about the door with the saying on it. The numbers on the map had meant nothing much, they were the co-ordinates of the island itself. They weren't sure what the peacocks that were drawn on the clock tower meant. They looked at the peacocks drawn on the broken clock. "Peacocks, clocks, and time, these are the clue items, but we don't know what the link is," Omari said. It was like a symbol for time, since the original map was also found in a clock. "Maybe it's not a clue to the map." Omari suggested. "Perhaps it's a message for the person that finds it, that we need to strive and work hard for success, and that we should make use of our time. That time is of the essence," Omari emphasized. Bakari agreed and added, "Maybe the ticking of the clock reminds us that our life is ticking away and that we have to benefit from the time, by being productive".

Bakari read the poem again, that he had written in his notebook. He read it once and then repeated some of the verses as if contemplating the meaning:

…Is to believe you can

Say "I can"

"Yes Omari," he continued, "You could be right. It is like the poem is telling us not just to work hard to achieve success in life but to also believe that you can. To believe in yourself and that you can do it." The boys felt as if they were in an English Literature class, where they had to analyse a poem. Bakari made a list of all the keywords. He felt that perhaps if all the keywords were together, the clue would become apparent. He told Omari to help him write the list:

Peacocks

Clocks

Time

Say 'I can'

Strive for success

Bakari scratched his head. He really could not make out anything from the keywords. He decided to write down how everything had linked up:

Clock

Ruby

Map

Strive for success

Prison Island

Peacocks

Door – Strive for success (with peacock drawing)

Clock tower (with peacock drawing)

"Maybe there is no physical treasure like the rubies but the treasure of life is to succeed," Omari philosophised. "Yes," agreed Bakari. He remembered a quote by Mother Teresa that he had memorised in school, "Yesterday is gone. Tomorrow has not yet come. We have only today. Let us begin." The boys fell silent for a few minutes.

"Yes, oh well, at least we tried and thought we could help Bibi Fatuma by finding the rubies and selling them," said Bakari. "Well, it doesn't mean we can't help her. Let's think of something or somehow we can help her save her business," he added feeling empowered with the words of the poem. Bakari said, "Say, I can!" Omari repeated after Bakari, "Yes, I can!" Mzee Kasuku also joined in and kept saying, "Yes I can, yes I can, yes I can, yes I can…" until Bakari and Omari had to bribe him with nuts to stop. "Yes, Mzee Kasuku, we totally believe you. We believe that you can!" Omari joked and both the boys burst out into laughter.

Chapter Thirteen

Bayt-el-Jameel

Bakari and Omari climbed down the tree house to go to speak to Bibi Fatuma. When they reached the lounge, they saw her sitting on her sofa looking gloomy. Captain Cook sat opposite her, grim-faced. There were two additional men sitting on the sofas, dressed in formal attire. As the boys approached the group, the two unknown men stood up to leave. They all shook hands and one of them said, "We hope things work out for you Bibi Fatuma. It has been good doing business with you. We'll take good care of the house." They turned around to leave. Bakari and Omari stood at the door, their eyes widened out of curiosity. Bibi Fatuma saw the boys standing near the door and gestured for them to come in and sit down. They greeted her and Captain Cook. "I'm sorry that I have not been able to save Bayt-el-Jameel, Bibi Fatuma," said Captain Cook, "But we had to save either Bayt-el-Jameel or your business. And hopefully the money will return with the business." The boys exchanged glances and then turned to Bibi Fatuma. She had lowered her head as if it was too much for her. The realisation of Captain Cook's words slowly sank in. Bayt-el-Jameel had already been sold. They had not been able to help. They sat there as if frozen.

Just then, Captain Cook's phone rang and he excused himself, leaving the room.

Bibi Fatuma looked up in the boys' direction. A tear had rolled down her cheek but she was smiling. She gestured for the boys to come and sit near her. "Bakari, Omari," she started. "I had to sell Bayt-el-Jameel in order to save my business. The men that you saw here were lawyers of Captain Cook's friend, who will be buying Bayt-el-Jameel. They have been generous to me and allowed me to stay here until the paperwork is completed. They will transfer the money into my business account within a month. Captain Cook is assiting with putting together the agreement for the house sale. Things will be different from now on boys. We have to be strong and face the reality of the situation," she spoke softly, as if consoling herself. Bakari still could not believe that she had full trust in Captain Cook.

"I will stay in Zanzibar until everything is settled," she concluded. She was now looking at her hands and talking. "Is there anyway left to save the house, Bibi Fatuma?" Bakari asked. She shook her head. A proverb came to Bakari's mind, "Everything is okay in the end, if it's not okay, then it's not the end," he said to Bibi Fatuma. If things were not okay then this was definitely not the end, there must be a way. Captain Cook walked into the lounge and cleared his throat as he spoke, "The lawyers will draw up the final papers and you only have to sign them." Bibi Fatuma was too tired to question. She nodded her head and replied weakly, "yes." The room went quiet. Everyone was absorbed in their thoughts until Bakari broke the silence and asked, "May I see the agreement?"

Bibi Fatuma looked up curiously at Bakari thinking she had misheard him. "The what?" she asked. "The agreement Bibi

Fatuma, for selling the house. May I see it?" Both Bibi Fatuma and Omari looked at Bakari as if he had gone mad. Bakari's gut feeling about Captain Cook had become stronger. He had to find someone who could help him read the agreement and see if it was sound. He didn't want to tell Bibi Fatuma about his plan yet, as already she was too tired and upset. Also, Bakari worried that she would laugh at the thought that he distrusted Captain Cook. Bibi Fatuma smiled encouragingly.

"Can you please give the boys a copy of the agreement," she said to Captain Cook who looked at Bakari in the eye. "Why? What do you want to see?" he asked sounding cold. "I'm just curious to read the agreement and see that everything is okay," Bakari retorted. When Bibi Fatuma couldn't see his face, Captain Cook raised his eyebrows and rolled his eyes, as if mocking Bakari. "Sure Bakari," he said smiling. The smile looked very sarcastic. Captain Cook reached for his top pocket and took out some folded papers. "Here, this is the draft that I have," he said and then turned to Bibi Fatuma to excuse himself. "I have some urgent matters regarding the business I need to take care of," he said with an air of pride and left the room. Bibi Fatuma did not seem to notice the pride in his voice nor the way he had rolled his eyes sarcastically at Bakari. The more Bakari thought about Captain Cook, the more he felt that there was something not right about him. He had to listen to his intuition. Why was Bibi Fatuma so obedient to Captain Cook? She was not like that with anyone else. She gave orders and everyone obeyed. However, with Captain Cook around, it seemed like she took orders. He had to figure out what was going on and save Bibi Fatuma and a family heirloom. He and Omari had to figure a way to save Bibi Fatuma's house. His instinct told him that it was still not too late.

Chapter Fourteen

The Agreement

Bakari and Omari opened the copy of the agreement that Captain Cook had given them. They had to go over it themselves and see if they could understand it. The legal terminologies were very difficult for them to grasp. Even if they sat with a dictionary, they found it hard to understand the words. "We need to show it to someone who would understand these legal words and phrases," Bakari proposed. Omari clicked his fingers. He had an idea, "Let's take it to your father. I'm sure he's is good with all this legal stuff." Bakari agreed, "Yes, Baba could go over it and tell us if there is anything odd in the agreement." He continued to flip over the pages. It was titled, 'Agreement of Sale' and under this was 'Terms and Conditions'. On the last page, there were dotted lines to be signed on. There were already signatures on it. That means the deal was already done. One of the signatures was of a Mr. Borris Vendukal. It said 'buyer' under his name. Bibi Fatuma's signature was under 'seller'. That much was simple to understand. There was another thing that caught Bakari's attention but at that moment he didn't think much of it.

Bakari and Omari went to Baba with the agreement. He read over it and said it appeared fine to him. He dismissed the idea that Bakari should take it to a lawyer to read. "Captain Cook is a trustworthy man Bakari, he has shown it to his lawyers and we know he would do the right thing," Baba said. "But Baba, what if…" interrupted Bakari. "Bakari!" Baba stopped him in the middle of his sentence, "I have also read it over and it seems fine to me. Besides, the deal has already been done!" Bakari wanted to keep arguing but one look from his father and he thought it best not to. The boys were disappointed. They had hoped Baba would have understood them and helped prove that Captain Cook was indeed a dishonest and shady person. But Baba didn't want to talk further on the matter.

The boys talked about the map and told him about all the clues they had found and what they thought so far. He agreed with them that it must have only been a message to the person who finds it, that in order to succeed in life one must strive hard and not waste any precious time.

The boys returned to their tree house. They knew they had a limited amount of time left to use it and wanted to make the most of it. Bakari trusted his father but for some reason his father also trusted Captain Cook and did not doubt his intentions. They had made the tree house their secret meeting place where they were sure no one would hear their conversations. "Bakari, I think you have no reason to distrust Captain Cook. Everyone else seems to trust him," Omari argued. Bakari decided to be logical, "Look Omari, even if I agree that he is trustworthy there is no harm in checking the agreement over more thoroughly so we know he has not omitted anything important. Think of it as our way to help

Bibi Fatuma". Omari didn't disagree on that point. "Let's find a lawyer then," he said, "He will be objective as he wouldn't know anyone personally involved in the deal." Bakari agreed, "True, no harm in that, but…" he paused, "Where will we get the money to pay a lawyer?" The boys knew that lawyers charged hefty fees even for a ten-minute consultation. Bakari had not thought of that. "Okay," he said, "Let's think about it."

As the boys sat in the tree house, thinking of a way to earn some money for the lawyers' fees, Omari suddenly snapped his fingers. He had an idea. "Why don't we go to Mr. Punda, our Economics teacher? I'm sure he could figure out a way for us," he said excitedly. Bakari thought it was a great idea as well, "Yes! Mr. Punda will surely help!"

They decided to photocopy the agreement for Mr. Punda so they could also keep a copy. They got on their bicycles and cycled towards their school. It was holiday time so the school was empty. Mr. Punda lived in the teachers' quarters behind the school building. As they approached the gate they saw he was about to leave on his motorbike. They waved at him and he waved back. They were out of breath as they reached him. "Mr. Punda, we were looking for you," Omari said almost panting. Mr. Punda had a worried look on his face. "Is everything okay?" he enquired. The boys explained about Bibi Fatuma's house being sold and that they wanted to make sure that the agreement was correct but could not afford to pay a lawyer. "Can you have a look at the agreement and see if everything is okay?" Bakari pleaded.

Mr. Punda hesitated, then looked at his watch. "I need to go somewhere now but if you'd like, leave the agreement with me, and I will go through it when I come back. You can call me in the evening," he said. The boys were grateful for his kind gesture. They left the copy of the agreement with him, took his phone number, and rode back to Stone Town. They had to be patient and wait for the evening before they could call him. They saw one of their friends walking along the road. "*Salama* Yahya," Bakari and Omari greeted him. "*Habari yako* Yahya," added Mzee Kasuku. Yahya greeted them back and offered Mzee Kasuku a tomato from his bag. He had bought some vegetables for his mother and was on his way home. "Don't forget, we're going to Jambiani beach on Wednesday," he reminded them. Of course! Bakari and Omari had forgotten about their day at the beach. During the holidays, they frequently went to spend a whole day at different beaches with a large group of their school friends. "Sure, Yahya," replied Bakari. "Thanks for the reminder, we will see you on Wednesday!" Omari said waving at Yahya.

The boys headed towards Forodhani Gardens to get away from the late afternoon sun. They threw themselves on the grass and lay down on their backs. Bakari pulled out his copy of the agreement to look at it again. Omari glanced at him and said, "Bakari just have the patience. It's not like we can understand all those technical terms!" However there was something Bakari had seen on the paper that had caught his attention earlier. He had not mentioned it so far because he wanted to see if anyone else noticed. The signatures on the dotted lines were meant to be by two different people but they appeared in the same hand writing. The second signature had a date scribbled next to it, 31st June, whereas the first signature did not have anything besides it. Did that mean that only one person had signed it? Had Bibi Fatuma really signed these papers? He decided he would be patient until Mr. Punda gave them his comments.

ın the evening, the boys called Mr. Punda using Omari's cell phone. "You can come over now boys, I've had a look at the agreement," Mr. Punda said over the phone. The boys hurried to their bikes and as quick as lightning peddled their way to Mr. Punda's building. "The conditions and terms all seem to be in order," he said. Bakari was rather disappointed. He had thought maybe Mr. Punda would have picked something up. "What about the signatures Mr. Punda? Does it look like only one person has signed them?" Bakari asked. Mr. Punda looked closely at the signatures. It looks like both the people signed it using one pen. Both of their signatures appear simple," he said, "the purchaser is a Mr. Borris Vendukal of Switzerland and the seller is Bibi Fatuma". That part had been obvious to the boys, but they were scrutinising everything on the agreement. "Funnily the date has been written wrong but I'm sure the lawyers will correct this on the final draft," he added.

Bakari and Omari thanked Mr. Punda and rode back to Forodhani Gardens. They each ordered a mug of sugarcane juice with Zanzibar mix. As they sat down to eat, both were lost in thought, "What are you thinking Bakari?" Omari enquired. "Let's eat first and then we'll discuss." When they were done, Bakari said. "Look at the date Omari," pointing at the agreement. "I actually had noticed this earlier but was waiting to see what Mr. Punda thought." Omari took the agreement and looked at where the date was scribbled. He then nodded and said, "True, Bakari, this is an official document, there can be no mistake. There are not thirty-one days in June. How can the person who signed it make such a grave mistake?" Bakari clicked his fingers and pointed out, "How does Mr. Borris of Switzerland and Bibi Fatuma have a similar simple signature? And also, when was this document signed by him? See, I told you, what we need to do now is find out who this purchaser is? Who is Mr. Borris Vendukal?"

Chapter Fifteen

Mr. Borris Vendukal

Omari and Bakari decided to ask their friend Mr. Google for information on Mr. Borris Vendukal. The agreement had Mr. Borris' full name and an address in Switzerland. That would be a starting point in finding out who he was. They cycled to the Internet café and typed in the name Borris Vendukal. There were no results. Perhaps Mr. Borris wasn't famous or rich. They typed the street name that was on the agreement. 47 Avenue Blanc, Geneva, Switzerland. There were many results on Google. "Well, it seems Mr. Borris is more famous than we thought. Look how many results have come up," Bakari said. But as Omari clicked on the first result, it showed that that was the address for the Tanzanian Embassy in Geneva in Switzerland. "Maybe Mr. Borris works there?" Omari thought. "Maybe that's why he's given the embassy address?" he added. Bakari scratched his head and said, "It doesn't sound right. Something strange is going on here.

How can we find out whether this Mr. Borris Vendukal works at the Tanzanian Embassy in Switzerland and whether he really bought Bibi Fatuma's house? We should contact them, someone must know who this Mr. Borris Vendukal is." They searched for numbers of the Swiss Embassy in Dar es Salaam and the Tanzanian Embassy in Switzerland. It was easy to find the numbers with the help of Mr. Google. The number appeared and they decided to call. "Can I please speak to Mr. Borris Vendukal," Bakari asked. "Mr. who?" replied the voice on the other side. "We're sorry but we have no Mr. Vendukal working here for us," said the voice over the phone. Bakari hung up the phone. "No Mr. Vendukal there," he told Omari. "We need to call the Geneva number and ask for a Mr. Vendukal there," Omari suggested. They looked at the time, now it was late afternoon. They would have to try to call tomorrow morning. They decided to use their mobile phone to make the long distance call; it would be cheaper than a public phone.

The next morning they called the Tanzanian Embassy in Geneva. A friendly woman picked up the phone and spoke in a foreign language. When she realised the caller was speaking in English, she switched languages, "How may I help you sir?" she asked politely. "Hello, I am looking for a Mr. Borris Vendukal," Omari asked confidently. "Where are you calling from and what is it regarding?" she asked in a crisp and cheery voice. Omari's eyes widened, now what do I say, he thought. "This is an urgent call from Tanzania for Mr. Boris Vendukal," Omari said in his utmost formal voice. There was a pause on the other side. Then, the woman spoke again, "I am putting you through, Sir."

A chill ran down Omari's spine. What if there really was a Mr. Borris Vendukal, what would he say to him? Omari nudged Bakari. "There is a Mr. Vendukal. What should I say to him?" he asked nervously, covering the phone microphone with his hand. Bakari quickly said, "Put the phone on loudspeaker so we can both hear!" The phone was still ringing on the other side. Then someone picked up and spoke in a deep voice, "Hello, how can I help you?" Omari panicked and was lost for words, so Bakari took over the phone and quickly thought of something to say. He put on his most formal voice, "Yes, hello Mr. Vendukal. I am calling in regards to your purchasing of a property in Zanzibar…" The deep voice interrupted Bakari, "I'm sorry. I am Mr. Vendukal's assistant, he has travelled to Zanzibar to see the property. I am sure you can meet him there." "Oh, I see," Bakari said, "Can you please tell us when he travelled here as we need to close the deal," Bakari said. "He has been there since last week," informed the man with the deep voice. "The seller may offer the house to another interested buyer and we need to urgently call him, can you please give his number here in Zanzibar?" Bakari asked, trying to make his voice as deep as he could, hoping he would sound older.

The man with the deep voice was hesitant. He paused for a moment. Bakari could imagine him scratching his head. "Can I get your number and pass it on to Mr. Vendukal?" he finally replied. Oh no! Bakari thought. That's it! Plan failed. He opened his eyes wide at Omari, hoping his friend would help him deal with the situation. Witty as he was, Bakari quickly thought of a response, "We had his contact and have somehow misplaced his number. We would rather have his number so we can contact him immediately. If you cannot give out his details, we understand. Please then tell Mr. Vendukal that it is unfortunate we could not do business with him. Thank you for your assistance," he spoke as casually and confidently as his voice would allow him to sound. The assistant hesitated again. Bakari now imagined him sweating profusely. For a second Bakari thought that his idea hadn't worked and started thinking of a different way to get hold of Mr. Vendukal's number when the assistant's voice cut through his thoughts. "You can try this number," he said and proceeded to read out a local number for Mr. Vendukal in Zanzibar. Omari quickly jotted it down.

After they hung up, Omari said, "This doesn't mean much. Maybe Captain Cook did meet with Mr. Vendukal and he signed the agreement paper." It was a possibility Bakari thought; Bibi Fatuma had left all the matters in Captain Cook's hands. "Still, we should meet him," Bakari said.

They walked towards Bayt-el-Jameel and saw Bibi Fatuma and Captain Cook talking in soft voices. Bibi Fatuma glanced up and saw the boys. She gestured them to come and sit next to them. When Captain Cook saw the boys he asked in a sarcastic voice, "Did you boys go over the agreement then? Is everything okay?" The boys smiled at him but didn't answer.

Bakari turned towards Bibi Fatuma and asked, "Bibi Fatuma, have you met the buyer for the house?" Captain Cook looked shocked at Bakari's sudden authority. Bibi Fatuma shook her head. "He is not in this country," she said. Then Bakari turned to Captain Cook and asked, "Captain Cook, who is this man who is purchasing my Bibi Fatuma's house?" Captain Cook looked annoyed at being asked such an absurd question by a small boy. "He's a friend of mine and he is helping us by buying this house," he responded. "When did he sign the papers?" Bakari queried, glaring at Captain Cook. "He signed them a day after Bibi Fatuma," Captain Cook replied. Bibi Fatuma was suddenly more fascinated than annoyed with Bakari's interest and she let him ask the questions as a man representing her family. "Did he come to Zanzibar to sign the papers?" Bakari further interrogated. "Of course he did," Captain Cook responded, sounding more annoyed. "So where is he now?" Bakari asked.

"He's still here," Captain Cook replied. "Well, please invite him over for tea later on today. I'm sure Bibi Fatuma would like to meet him since he's been so kind to allow her to stay till the paperwork is finished," Bakari said sounding rather sarcastic.

Captain Cook looked concerned and turned to look at Bibi Fatuma. Bibi Fatuma smiled at Captain Cook and said, "Yes, why not? I've met his lawyers, I would like to meet him too." Bakari felt that Bibi Fatuma was too dazed to notice what was going on. She didn't even know that the buyer was in Zanzibar. Why had Captain Cook not informed Bibi Fatuma of that? Had he thought it was irrelevant for her to know? Or was it because he didn't want Bibi Fatuma to know who the buyer was? If that was so, what was he afraid of? Captain Cook nodded his head, "I will arrange that," he said and with that he walked out of the house.

In the evening, as Bakari and Omari had expected, Captain Cook didn't bring the guest, "He couldn't make it Bibi Fatuma. He sends his apologies." Bibi Fatuma didn't think anything of the matter and calmly accepted his apologies.

The boys however sensed that something strange was happening. They decided to find out what was going on. Why did Captain Cook not want Bibi Fatuma to meet the buyer? The boys thought of a plan. They dialled Mr. Vendukal's number from a phone booth. Omari put a cloth on the receiver end to muffle his voice. The phone rang and a man picked up. "Hello," he said. "Hello," replied Omari, trying to change his voice and accent as much as he could. "Is this Mr. Vendukal?" "Yes it is," replied the man. "We have something that may interest you," Omari said. "Yes? What would that be?" Mr. Vendukal asked. "A treasure and a huge ruby!" Omari said, emphasising each word. "Who are you?" Mr. Vendukal asked, "And how do I know that you really have these?" "We can meet at the lobby of Tembo

Hotel this evening," suggested Bakari. At this point, all what the boys wanted was to see who this Mr. Vendukal was, they weren't really interested in meeting him. Mr. Vendukal hesitated for a moment and Bakari felt as if he was uncertain of meeting the boys. Maybe Bakari had it all wrong. Just then, Mr. Venduakal spoke and said, "I will meet you outside the House of Wonders at seven tonight." Bakari was confused. Why did Mr. Vendukal want to meet them outside the House of Wonders at night instead of a hotel reception in front of people? "It's a deal," Omari said, "How will we recognise you?" Omari asked. He didn't wait for Mr. Vendukal to respond, "Come holding a book in your left hand," and with that Omari hung up.

Half an hour after sunset, the boys hid away under a tree, a spot where the House of Wonders was in full view to them. They left Mzee Kasuku at home this time. They didn't want to be easily spotted with a parrot. A man wearing a black suit walked towards the side gate. He was tall and had a big build. From the distance, his big stomach made him look like he was pregnant. He took out a book from his pocket and held it in his left hand. He walked under a streetlight and the boys noticed the man had a scar on his face and was clean shaven. He stood by the gate, looking everywhere, his eyes darting in all directions. He was searching for someone. The boys were shocked at who they saw under the streetlight. It was Captain Cook! Why was Captain Cook posing as Mr. Vendukal? Omari nudged Bakari and asked the obvious, "Why is Captain Cook here instead of Mr. Vendukal?" Bakari crossed his brows and gave Omari a look of bewilderment. The boys left before they could be spotted, both thinking the same thing, why did Captain Cook come instead of Mr. Vendukal?

Chapter Sixteen

Jambiani

The boys still could not believe Captain Cook had arrived instead of Mr. Borris Vendukal. How could that be? Could it be because Mr. Vendukal had asked Captain Cook to come to the meeting place since they were friends? Why didn't Mr. Vendukal want to appear himself? What was he hiding? How would the boys ever find out?

"Why do you think Captain Cook came instead of Mr. Vendukal?" Omari asked at last, having had enough of debating the question in his mind. "It's so strange Omari! Really! Mr. Vendukal refuses to meet us at the reception of a hotel, he suggests a meeting in the dark in a 'secret' place and then he doesn't even turn up!" Bakari said it all in one breath. "I think we need to talk to someone about this," Omari concluded. They decided to tell an adult about it. They preferred confiding in Baba rather than Bibi Fatuma as they felt she was in a vulnerable position. She was so heartbroken with her house being sold and might not be able to understand the boys' concern. Unfortunately, Baba had travelled to Dar es Salaam for a day on some business. He was due back in the evening.

The boys remembered it was Wednesday and they had promised to spend the day at the beach with their friends. "It's Wednesday and we are supposed to go to the beach with Yahya and the others. Let's go enjoy the sun and sea. By the time we're back, Baba should also be home". "Okay," Omari agreed, "We better go to Yahya's place before they start looking for us," he added. They quickly grabbed their swimming costumes, towels, and packed some snacks before leaving. They would join a group of their friends in Jambiani to play football and spend the day on the beach.

Jambiani was a village located about forty kilometres from Stone Town and the group had hired two private *daladala*'s for the day. There were over thirty-five boys, each paid out of his pocket for the trip. To hire a *daladala* was relatively inexpensive and the boys always saved money from their weekly pocket expense for such day trips. Most of them carried snacks and drinks for the day on the beach.

Omari and Bakari decided to bring Mzee Kasuku as well and he seemed excited to be in a *daladala* full of boys. He quietly observed the boys first and listened to their conversation. Then out of excitement he started repeating everything he had heard and could not stop making noise. The boys found him amusing. "What a cool parrot," some of them praised Mzee Kasuku. He had everyone's attention on the bus and made them laugh throughout the journey. All the boys now wanted to own a funny parrot like Mzee Kasuku.

The group arrived in Jambiani and headed straight for the beach. There were a lot of fishermen that day, some were still out in the sea, some had arrived on the shore and were heading towards the village, some more were sitting on the beach fixing their nets.

The boys left their belongings on the beach near to where the fishermen were. They found a spot far from the fishermen, and started to gather sticks and stones to create goalposts. Having divided themselves into teams, the game began.

They played until they felt they needed a break. When they came towards their clothes, they found that some of their things were missing. Bakari and Omari also couldn't find Mzee Kasuku. "What if someone stole Mzee Kasuku!" Bakari said with worry. Just then, they heard a sound of laughter. They looked up to a nearby coconut tree that had its trunk twisted and low down. Mzee Kasuku was sitting on one of the boy's shirts and had pulled another shirt over his head. He was trying to pull all the clothes on the trunk of a tree! "He's such a prankster!" laughed Bakari.

Mzee Kasuku realised that the boys were watching him. He walked briskly towards them leaving the shirt on the branch, took someone's sunglasses and attempted to balance them on his head rather unsuccessfully. "What a clown!" one of the boys shouted. Mzee Kasuku loved the attention. He showed them some more tricks. He held a tomato and started peeling it with his claws. The attention-seeking bird had gone through the boys' belongings while they were busy playing football. "Good food!" he said, making the boys crack up! The boys ran to the tree and grabbed their shirts from the lower branch. One of them said, "Mzee Kasuku, I'd never hire you as my guard again!" "Show-off," another boy added. This made all the boys laugh. Mzee Kasuku imitated their chuckle and sent the boys into another fit of laughter.

Some of the boys walked into town to buy ice-cold water and juice from the many small grocery shops. Some bought fried fish that was being sold on the streets. They sat down together on the beach and had a picnic. Then they went for a swim. The water was crystal clear. The tide was getting full and they swam deep into the sea. Normally when it was low tide, it was very easy to see the coral reef because it was so close to the shore.

When the boys got out they found that Mzee Kasuku had decided to come back down from the tree and sunbathe on the sand, again using someone's t-shirt to lie down on! "Shoo Mzee Kasuku!" said one of the boys. "Get off our clean t-shirts! You're making a mess," said another. "Shoo You! You Shoo!" replied Mzee Kasuku giving them a look, as if they had just disturbed him. He had attempted to put on the sunglasses again. This time he managed to keep them on but the glasses were too big for his small head and made him look ridiculous. He managed to get the boys in another laughing frenzy. Bakari and Omari still chuckling decided to go to the beach kiosk to buy water with Mzee Kasuku in tow.

As the sun started setting, the rest of the boys returned to the *daladalas* to go back to Stone Town. As they were in a rush to get home, they didn't realise that Mzee Kasuku, Omari, and Bakari, had not gotten onto the *daladala*. Since there were two *daladalas*, each group of boys assumed that they were on the other bus.

Suddenly, Omari and Bakari realised they had been left behind as they were returning from the kiosk. "Oh no!" Bakari shouted, "The *daladalas* left without us!" "Bummer! It looks like we will have to catch another bus!" Omari said. "Well, let's go change while we wait for another to come along," Bakari suggested. They went behind a tree to change while Mzee Kasuku waited for them on the top branch of a nearby tree. Suddenly two men appeared and pushed the boys against the tree trunk, covering their mouths with their hands. One held a knife against Omari's throat. What did these men want? One of them spoke in a harsh voice, "Hand over the ruby and the map?" Omari was stunned. How did these men know that they had a ruby and had found a treasure map? Who were they? Thank God I left the ruby at home today, Bakari thought as he kicked the man holding him on his shin. The man cried out in pain and held his leg. Mzee Kasuku flew down from the branch he had been sitting on and bit the man holding his shin with his sharp beak. Then he flew on the other man's shoulder and bit him hard on the nose. Mzee Kasuku flew back on top of the branch and shouted, "Fire! Fire! Fire! Both men were totally taken by surprise from the parrots attacks. At his cries, people from the nearby village began to gather to see what the commotion was about.

The man holding on Omari loosened his grip and held his nose where he had been bitten. This gave both Omari and Bakari and opportunity to run from the men. The boys ran at full speed towards the village knowing the attackers would not pursue them in front of the villagers. Mzee Kasuku flew above the boys. They had to get back to Stone Town before the bandits found them again.

Their only option was catching the next daladala on the main road. They quickly ran towards the road and were in luck, as a bus was just dropping off passengers, when they reached. Bakari proceeded to enter the bus with Mzee Kasuku clutching him tightly on his shoulder and Omari close behind.

They had no idea who the men that had attacked them were. How did they know that Bakari and Omari had found a ruby and a treasure map? How had they known they were in Jambiani? All what the boys knew was that they were in danger and they had to find help! As soon as the bus stopped, they leapt out and headed home. Thankfully, Baba had arrived back from

Dar es Salaam. They rushed into the house to tell him what had happened. When he saw them out of breath and the worried looks on their faces, he knew something was wrong. He took them inside and tried to calm them down.

"Baba, there were two men, and they had a knife and we were stranded and they knew about our map and…" Bakari said without stopping for breath.

"Calm down Bakari. Sit down and have some water first," Baba said trying to calm the boys down. "We were at the beach in Jambiani and these two men must have followed us. They attacked us and asked for the ruby and the treasure map," Bakari recounted. Baba was confused. How could anyone know about the map if the boys hadn't told anyone about it? The boys then started to tell them about Mr. Vendukal. How they had called him and told him that they had found a ruby and a map.

"Baba, you know we suspect Captain Cook," Omari continued. Bakari's father looked confused again. "What has Captain Cook got to do with any of this?" he asked. The boys explained how Captain Cook had come for the rendezvous instead of Mr. Vendukal and how he wanted to meet them secretly rather than at a hotel reception. They told him that they were suspicious of Mr. Vendukal and Captain Cook. Why hadn't Mr. Vendukal come for tea at Bibi Fatuma's while he was in Zanzibar? In addition, the signature signed on the contract papers had an incorrect date, the 31st of June.

"Well boys, maybe it's time we found out why Mr. Vendukal doesn't want to show us his face," Baba proposed, "And whether it was him who sent the men to attack you." Baba had a close friend who was a police officer, Mr. Kawe. He suggested the boys go to see him immediately. "Mr. Kawe will be the best person to advise us," said Baba. "He can advise us on what legal steps we could take and how to report the attack".

Chapter Seventeen

Mr. Borris Vendukal and Captain Cook

When Baba and the boys arrived at Mr. Kawe's house, he was just returning from the mosque. He was happy to see Baba and the boys. "What an honour to have the 'Detectives of Shangani' come to my house!" he teased.

Baba gestured to Mr. Kawe that they had something important to tell him, "Abasi, there's something you need to know," Baba said addressing Mr. Kawe by his first name, in a tone that showed urgency. Mr. Kawe knew straight away that all was not well.

He led them inside the house and into a small room at the back of the house, "What's wrong Musa?" he enquired. Baba told the boys to relate the attack that had happened and everything they knew about Mr. Vendukal. Mr. Kawe listened attentively, holding his chin and scratching his head. "We need to catch the attackers. We cannot tolerate any danger to our children on this island!" Mr. Kawe said with a serious look on his face. "I'm sure Mr. Vendukal will be able to tell us who the men were, since he was the only other person who knew about the ruby and the map. Captain Cook can lead us to Mr. Vendukal.

We cannot wait until morning lest the attackers get away. We need to take action now," he said standing up. He turned towards the boys, "You two stay here," he ordered. However, the boys were eager to follow and see what happens. "Can we please join you?" Bakari pleaded. Mr. Kawe wasn't sure and looked at Baba for guidance. Both Omari and Bakari made long sad faces, hoping Mr. Kawe would change his mind. Mr. Kawe gave a heartily laugh. "Okay detectives, you can join us," he said. "Yes!" the boys shouted in chorus. Mzee Kasuku repeated after the boys, "Yes, yes yes!" "Very well then, the detectives' parrot can join us as well!" Mr. Kawe repeated with a smile. He made a few phone calls and arranged for two added police cars to come and pick them all up. They were going to Bayt-el-Jameel first to find Captain Cook. They needed to ask him more about Mr. Vendukal.

The police officers first decided to search Bayt-el-Jameel in case Captain Cook had gone there. When Baba and the boys entered the house with the police, Bibi Fatuma was worried. "Is everything okay? Why are the police here? What happened?" she asked. "We're looking for Mr. Vendukal and we hope Captain Cook can tell us where to find him," explained Mr. Kawe. Baba and the boys pulled Bibi Fatuma aside and quickly explained to her what had happened. She was shocked. How could someone attack the boys for a ruby? However, she dismissed the idea that Mr. Vendukal or Captain Cook would know what was going on. She thought it must be thugs who had overheard Omari or Bakari talking about their treasure map. She paused for a second, as if recalling something, "Actually I may have mentioned to Captain Cook about the ruby you found from the clock and how I told you to throw it away," she said. "Aha!" said Bakari, "So Captain Cook *does* know we have the ruby." Bakari wondered that maybe he also knew it was Omari and Bakari who made the phone call asking for Mr. Vendukal to meet at the hotel reception.

Captain Cook was not at Bayt-el-Jameel. The police needed to locate where he was. They found that he was staying in a hotel in Stone Town and went to the receptionist to enquire. The receptionist looked through the hotel register and informed them that there was no one by the name of Captain Cook there, but there was a Mr. Vendukal. The receptionist took the police to Mr. Vendukal's room and knocked. Captain Cook answered. He was nervous when he saw the police outside the room. "We're looking for Mr. Vendukal," Mr. Kawe demanded, his voice full of authority. "Mr. Vendukal has just stepped out of the room," Captain Cook explained. Mr. Kawe ordered his team to search the room. "Please step out of the room Captain Cook, we have a few questions to ask you while we wait for Mr. Vendukal to return," Mr. Kawe demanded.

Captain Cook was dressed in a bathrobe and asked if he could go in and change. Mr. Kawe refused. "It won't take long," he said. "Do you have a permit to come into my room?" Captain Cook asked raising his eyebrows. Mr. Kawe didn't bother to respond. He led Captain Cook to a table at the further side of the hotel. There were not many people there. Two policemen stood behind Captain Cook. One sat down next to Captain Cook and Mr. Kawe with a notepad and pen. He was writing down everything that was being said. "Who is Mr. Vendukal?" Mr. Kawe asked. "He's a friend, who's come for a holiday here," answered Captain Cook sounding nervous. "A holiday? Or business?" Mr. Kawe asked. "Oh, a bit of both," Captain Cook blurted out uneasily.

Just then, one of the police officers who had been searching Mr. Vendukal's room came to call Mr. Kawe. "I think you'd like to see this," he said. Mr. Kawe got up and let the other police officer continue with the interrogation. The boys and Baba followed Mr. Kawe. When they entered the room, the police officer showed them two passports that he had found. One was an Omani passport and had a photo of Captain Cook with the name, 'Sher Shah Khan' written on it. The other also had a photo of Captain Cook and it had the name, 'Mr. Borris Vendukal' written there. It was a Swiss passport! "Oh my gosh! Captain Cook is Mr. Vendukal!" gasped Bakari. "I knew there was something fishy about him!" "That explains a lot," Omari said, "That is why he didn't bring Mr. Vendukal to meet Bibi Fatuma and why he came to the meeting place that evening himself." Bakari had thought the same thing. "He must have sent the bandits after us in Jambiani." Bakari concluded. "Because we were getting in his way and ruining his plan!" Omari continued.

"Well, we still have to find out what his motives are," Mr. Kawe said. He told the police officers to look for more evidence. He walked towards Captain Cook and said, "Nice plan Mr. Vendukal, alias Mr. Sher Shah Khan, alias Captain Cook! But you've just been caught. You are under arrest! Take him to the police station," he ordered the police officers. "We can interrogate him more there, and discover his whole plan," he added. Captain Cook tried to defend himself, "But, but, I am Sher Shah Khan and I hold a legal passport, and, and..." Mr. Kawe held out his hand in front of him, "You can explain yourself at the police station. I'm sure you have something interesting to tell us why you hold two passports with different names!"

The police led him to the room and let him change into his normal clothes, not letting him out of their sight or to touch anything in the room. They then led him to the police car. Meanwhile Mzee Kasuku shrieked loudly, "Captain Cook is a Crook! Captain Cook is a Crook!"

Mr. Kawe drove Baba and the boys to Bayt-el-Jameel. Bibi Fatuma was waiting there for them. She had been worried. Mr. Kawe, Baba, and the boys came in to tell her what they had discovered about Captain Cook. Mzee Kasuku also added his bit, "Captain Cook is a Crook!" Captain Cook is a Crook!"

"What!" exclaimed Bibi Fatuma as she heard the story being recounted. She was stunned and visibly shaken. "But, he is so honest, such a good man. How is it possible that he turned out like this?" she lamented. She was trying to make sense of what she had just heard. She found it difficult to digest the information, "No, possibly there's some sort of a mistake. Maybe you have got the wrong person," she said defending Captain Cook. "Bibi Fatuma! It is Captain Cook who has been trying to pollute your mind and fill it with lies regarding your property and business. He is not an honest man," Bakari articulated for Bibi Fatuma. It took a while until Bibi Fatuma was able to accept the information. She realised she had trusted him far too much; she had trusted him with everything she owned.

Mr. Kawe cleared his throat, "Bibi Fatuma, it's been a long day for everyone. Why don't you get some rest and we can talk about this in the morning," he advised.

Mzee Kasuku yawned as a sign that it was getting very late and that everyone should go to bed! Mr. Kawe said goodbye and told Bibi Fatuma he will pass by in the morning. Now that the boys were safe, they decided to stay over at Bibi Fatuma's to keep her company.

Chapter Eighteen

Captain Cook's Confession

At the police station, the officers had interrogated Captain Cook the entire night. They had given him the incentive that if he admitted the whole truth, then they would be able to help him out and lighten his sentence. He admitted everything. He told them that he was part of a syndicate that collected rare precious stones and properties. He was Bibi Fatuma's accountant but had businesses around the world. He admitted that he bought goods and property under Mr. Borris Vendukal's name as it was easier to deposit the money into the Swiss bank account.

It had been Captain Cook, over time, who had made her believe that all the bad things that happened to her were because of the stones she possessed. He had even orchestrated some bad events and had persuaded Bibi Fatuma that these things had happened due to her possession of the precious rocks. It was all to make her believe that she should not keep any. He had heard from some sources that there were hidden rubies somewhere in her house. He hoped that if he tricked Bibi Fatuma into selling the house, then it would give him the time to search every corner. Then Bibi Fatuma had mentioned about the boys finding a ruby from a clock they had accidentally

broken and discovered some silly map. Captain Cook wanted the ruby and the map from the boys and he had planned to take it from them. He also planned to kidnap the boys and hold them until he left Zanzibar, they were interfering too much with his plan.

Mr. Kawe came to Bibi Fatuma's in the later part of the morning to tell them what had happened and Captain Cook's confession. Bibi Fatuma, Omari, Bakari, and Bakari's parents were all waiting eagerly for him. "Captain Cook has admitted to many things. He was foolish enough to make a fake agreement so that he didn't have to pay a cent as part of his devious plan. Bibi Fatuma was a sweet old lady who trusted him completely, so he thought he would get away with anything and therefore became negligent. In this state of over confidence he had given Bakari the signed draft copy without even thinking. Both the signatures were his and the date was non-existent. Also, Bibi Fatuma's business was not failing but rather it was actually doing very well. Captain Cook had told of how he had amended the accounts to show her that the business was doing badly in the hope that she would agree to sell her house." Mr. Kawe gave all the updates on Captain Cook's confession to the eager listeners. Captain Cook also admitted to the secretary involvement in helping him.

When Omari and Bakari had called Geneva to find out Mr. Vendukal's number they had spoken to Henry who was also part of the syndicate. Henry had informed Captain Cook, who had then traced the number of the mobile phone the boys had called from. He had asked the vendors in the area if they had seen anyone near the House of Wonders that evening whose description had matched Omari and Bakari. He had sent two men to attack Omari and Bakari in Jambiani and get the map and ruby from them. The police were already searching for these two men.

As Bibi Fatuma listened to the story, she did not say much but showed her astonishment with her various facial expressions. She had hardly slept the previous night when Mr. Kawe had informed her of Captain Cook's fraudulence. Bibi Fatuma was a strong woman. Although she was very disappointed with the outcome of events, she believed there was a lesson to be learnt. Sometimes bad things happen to people so they can learn from it and gain the good from the bad. "Never put all your eggs in one basket," she said to herself, "Bibi Fatuma, you are never too old to learn!" Then her face changed as she thought of Captain Cook and how he had tried to deceive her and steal from her. "Aaah," she sighed, "How long can stolen goods last. Stolen goods have no blessing, the days of a robber are forty, the path of a liar is short, the path of a thief is short," she mumbled. Mr. Kawe asked Bibi Fatuma if she wanted to talk to Captain Cook and ask him anything. She told Mr. Kawe that she didn't want to see Captain Cook at all. She was not ready to see the evil man. She was grateful that God had saved her and thanks to the boys, she had discovered Captain Cook's true colours before it was too late.

"Thank you my boys," said Bibi Fatuma embracing Bakari and Omari, "I'm so glad I have detectives in my family!" she teased winking at them. "I shall always believe in your gut feelings," she told Bakari. They had saved her from the evil Captain Cook, and saved her house and had made her realise that her business was indeed thriving! Bibi Fatuma held Bakari and did a small dance with him, she opened her hand for Omari to join. Bakari had forgotten this jolly side of Bibi Fatuma. "This calls for a celebration!" Bibi Fatuma announced after having got over the initial shock of the news, "Tomorrow we shall have a grand feast and invite all our relatives and close friends." She added, "Enough food shall be cooked for the guests and more to be sent to all the orphanages in Zanzibar!"

She had come so close to losing everything and she had been blessed. She had to show her gratefulness.

The boys went to visit Mr. Kawe at the Police Station later during the day. They wanted to personally thank him for having helped them and saved Bibi Fatuma from a wretched man. The prison was a small place and the boys saw Captain Cook behind bars. They asked Mr. Kawe if they could say something to him. "Yes boys, you may if you like," responded Mr. Kawe.

The boys told Captain Cook about the map they had found. They told him the clue that was written on it: 'Man Jadda Wajada'. It was an advice about life; that the person who strives and works hard is successful at the end. Not by being a crook and a con artist! Captain Cook just stared ahead and did not say anything. Mzee Kasuku had heard Bibi Fatuma when she had been muttering to herself and he repeated everything she had said to Captain Cook, "Stolen goods have no blessing, the days of a robber are forty, the path of a liar is short, and the path of a thief is short." When they were about to leave, Mzee Kasuku made sure everyone knew what he thought of Captain Cook, "Captain Cook is a Crook! Captain Cook is a Crook!" he shouted at the top of his voice.

The boys thanked Mr. Kawe again as they left the police station. They headed for Bibi Fatuma's house and told her that Mzee Kasuku had given Captain Cook her messages. She laughed and patted Mzee Kasuku on his head. She got up from her armchair and hugged the boys. "This would not have been possible without the 'Detectives of Shangani.' Thank you so much. You have truly helped me in the best way possible. You have taught me to look at life with a different perspective," she said. The boys didn't know what to say. They felt overwhelmed that they had been able to help Bibi Fatuma this way.

Chapter Nineteen

The Feast and the Invisible Ink on the Map

It took Bibi Fatuma the whole night to comprehend the reality of the situation. She had believed she was at the verge of losing all her wealth. Now the realisation that she had not lost anything took time to sink in. In the morning, she had called her secretary in Oman and asked her to email all the accounts. She wanted to go through everything herself. She had arranged for someone to bring down the account book to her in Zanzibar. She had learnt from the boys that if she wanted success, she had to take action herself and not blindly rely on another person.

The first thing she was going to do was to replace the secretary. Anyone who had been working along with Captain Cook against her was definitely going to be fired!

Meanwhile, the servants were taking care of the preparations for the feast. Bakari and Omari were also running around helping set the tables for the guests. The guest list was not very long. Bibi Fatuma preferred it that way for today. She was happier that most of the food would go to the poor and the orphans. It was her way of saying thank you to God. She felt blessed.

The guests arrived and they all enjoyed the feast and had a cheerful evening. When the meal was over the guests had tea in the garden. By the time they left, the stars were shining bright. Finally, the only people remaining were Bibi Fatuma, Bakari, Omari, Mzee Kasuku, and Bakari's parents. They were just relaxing and enjoying each other's company. The boys started relating how they had figured out about Captain Cook. "Bakari didn't have a good feeling about him, from day one," Omari informed everyone. "When we spoke to a Mr. Vendukal and Captain Cook came instead, we knew that there was something wrong," Bakari said. Everyone had a question for the 'Detectives'. They sat together and the question session ran late into the night

Bakari still had the treasure map in his pocket. It was now crumpled and parts of the sides had fallen off. He knew it had meant nothing but it was a good advice on how to live life. He took it out of his pocket and showed it to Bibi Fatuma. Bibi Fatuma looked at the map and smiled. "Well you boys have given me my treasure," she said softly. Just then all the lights went out. There was a power cut. The maids quickly rushed into the rooms with candles. They placed them everywhere in the lounge. Bibi Fatuma passed the map back to Bakari. Bakari also looked at it again. As he was looking at it, Omari, who was lying down, noticed something at the back. He stared at the back of the map and his eyes widened. There was a candle nearby, he picked it up and moved it closer to the map. "What are you doing Omari? You will burn the map! Don't bring the candle so close!" Bakari shouted. But when he saw Omari's face he knew Omari had seen something. He turned the map around and lowered it so it was under the candle. He could not see what Omari had seen. So he lifted the map above the candle, far enough from the flame so it would not catch fire, and surely he saw what Omari had seen.

Gr.C and Her Fat Lock

'Gr.C and Her Fat Lock' had been written with an invisible ink! The invisible ink could only be seen when held over a candle. The writing appeared dirty and brown. The boys' mouths fell open with surprise! There was a clue. So perhaps the map was not just for advice? Maybe there was a treasure? The boys showed the clue to Bibi Fatuma and Bakari's parents. Bakari asked the question loudly, "Who's Gr C? And what does her fat lock mean? Is something hidden in a lock? What lock?" The bewildered boys looked at each other.

Bakari took out his notebook and opened where he had written all the keywords. Next to it he wrote down the new sentence:

Clock– peacocks
Ruby
Map
Strive for success
Prison Island
Peacocks
Door – Strive for success
Clock tower – peacocks
Gr.C and Her Fat Lock

He looked through his list and looked at what was the most common or recurring clue. It was peacocks and clocks. Maybe there was a lock in the clock? What or who was Gr.C? Maybe she had a lock in her clock somewhere? What did the peacocks have to do with a clock or a lock?

Bakari did what he always did, he tried to see if the words had a code or if they could be unscrambled to mean anything. He wrote down the words a few times and got many small words. He showed Omari what he was trying to do and together they unscrambled the word: grandfather clock!

Chapter Twenty

Grandfather Clock

The boys showed the word to Baba and Bibi Fatuma, 'Grandfather clock'. Bakari showed them the clues he had written before in his notebook. The clock they had broken, the clock of the House of Wonders, both had peacocks drawn on them. Just then the electricity returned. Bibi Fatuma thought about it for a minute, and then said, "You know, we have a grandfather clock that has peacocks on it too." The boys had heard the grandfather clock many times before. It was in the corner of the lounge. They were so used to it that they had never really looked at it, it was heard more than it was seen by most people. The boys walked over to the clock in the corner of the lounge. Bibi Fatuma and Bakari's parents followed. They were all curious to see if the unscrambled words really meant grandfather clock and whether it was this grandfather clock that was in the lounge. After all, Captain Cook had been convinced that the rubies were somewhere in Bayt-el-Jameel.

Bakari had never really looked at the clock from close up. Standing upright, tall and beautifully crafted, it stared at them. An antique piece of furniture that had been hidden in a corner, handcrafted especially for the Sultan, and passed down to

Bibi Fatuma through family generations. Standing taller than any of them, it added elegance and style to that part of the lounge. Its pendulum and weights were visible through a glass door. The brass hands and the Arabic numerals on the face showed that the clock was many years old. Intricate flowers were drawn at the corner. On either side of the face were two peacocks facing each other, just like on the door in the museum and the clock tower on the House of Wonders. What did that mean? "Maybe the rubies are hidden somewhere in this clock?" Omari thought aloud.

The pendulum swung and made a loud ticking noise. The wood case and glass were sparkling clean. The maids had polished the clock well to preserve its beauty.

"Bong! Bong! Bong!" Mzee Kasuku suddenly shouted giving everyone a fright. Bakari gave him an angry look. Mzee Kasuku laughed loudly. He was obviously looking for someone to play with.

The clock was placed right next to a wall hidden in a corner so they could not see what was at the back. They decided to try to move it so they could see what was behind. The clock was very heavy. All of them tried carefully to push the clock away from the wall. "No wonder it's in the corner. It's too heavy to move," Bakari said. They tried again. They pushed and they pulled, they dragged and heaved. Finally they managed to move it a little from the wall so that they could see the back of the clock. There was nothing there.

The clock had no legs, perhaps because the legs would not have been able to take its weight. The front part had a drawer but it did not open, it was only part of the design and drawing.

"Bibi Fatuma," Bakari said, "I know this may sound crazy but we need to break the bottom of this clock to see if the treasure is in here. We will never know otherwise. I'm sure we can fix the clock back later." He knew it was a tough decision for Bibi Fatuma, the grandfather clock had sentimental value for her. Bibi Fatuma did not think long before she answered with a smile, "I'm sure it can be fixed," she said. After all, Bakari and Omari had saved her from Captain Cook's evil plan, this was the least she could do to make them happy, even if they didn't find anything in the clock.

Bakari and Omari scratched their heads as to how to open the bottom with the least damage. Baba suggested removing it from the case first. He was familiar with it as he oversaw its repair whenever there was a problem with it. He lifted off the clock. He removed the weights and put them on a *khanga* he had asked Omari to bring. He did not want to damage the precious timepiece. Bakari also brought a toolbox and Baba took out a screwdriver and removed the screws that were securing the clock movement seat board. It was easy work for Baba as he had done this a few times before when adjusting the weights.

Once they had the clock and pendulum out safely, they started working at the bottom of the clock.

They tried to push it further from the wall. It was still heavy. They heaved and puffed while pulling and managed to move it a bit more. There were hidden screws at the bottom and Baba unscrewed them all. It would not be difficult to screw them back. Two of the bottom sides did not have screws and Baba decided it was necessary to cut through it. He looked through the toolbox and found a small long saw with a hard blade and a toothed edge. Since the two sides had opened with screws, he put the small sharp points of the blade and cut through the rest of the bottom. Baba did a clean job. He had cut straight and neatly. The bottom came off and he bent his head down to see what was inside. To his surprise, there was a metal box. He had hit it with his saw and it made a small sound. He took out a hammer from the toolbox and hit on the metal box. It made a loud noise. "This is what made the clock so heavy," he stated. They moved it still further away from the wall. They decided that if they tipped it over on its side, then the metal box would slide out, it was too heavy to try to carry it out.

Without the clock, pendulum and weights, it was easier to hold and move the empty case. They had to be careful as the metal box at the bottom of the clock made the bottom part heavier. They tried to move it by pushing the bottom part only; otherwise, it would crack in the middle.

They managed to tip it onto its side and the box slid out with a thud. The empty case felt light, the metal box had made it heavy.

When they managed to place the metal box facing them, they realised it was a safe! Bibi Fatuma gasped! Oh my gosh!, Could this be the hidden treasure of my great grandfather?

Chapter Twenty One

The Treasure

The safe was not only heavy but had a combination lock. "Well, this doesn't look good," Baba said, "These sorts of safes are very hard to open. Even drilling through this is difficult."

Bibi Fatuma used safes for her business in Oman, it was a common thing to keep money in, and she was familiar with dialling the combinations. "What could the combinations be?" Omari thought loudly. Bakari took out his notebook where he had written down everything. He saw nothing there that could be a number or turned into a number. He opened the map and looked at it again. There was nothing that they could use as a code. Omari leaned over to look at the map. He clicked his fingers and his eyes opened widely. "Oh my!" he exclaimed. What!" Bakari asked. "What have you noticed?" he repeated. Omari pointed at the co-ordinates that they had searched on Google for, they saw that it was the location for Zanzibar. "These are the only numbers there are. Let's see if it's a possibility that these are the combination numbers," he suggested. They showed the numbers to Bibi Fatuma, 5, 40, 6, 30, and 39. They were not sure whether these could be the numbers, but they had to try. There were five numbers on the treasure map. She started dialling the combination. She was very careful and turned the dial slowly and accurately. She knew that if she went past the exact number then she might have to start again.

Everyone was quiet. Even Mzee Kasuku realised he needed to be quiet. She turned the dial slowly to the right as she reached the last number; she put her ear close to the safe as if she wanted to hear something. The dial stopped itself and she heard a small click. On the first try, the lock cracked open.

The safe opened. Bibi Fatuma kneeled down to see what was in the safe. There was another small chest. Bibi Fatuma put her hands in the safe and lifted the chest, "*a kasha,*" she said softly. It was a beautiful chest with intricate carvings of flowers and brass ornamentations. She lifted the lid and took out a small book. The boys looked at each other. "That's it! The treasure is a book!" Bakari said loudly. Baba smiled, "Yes, maybe the secret of life is written in the book!" Bakari glanced at the title of the book and it surely read, "Secret to Life's success." Bakari knew that he and Omari would enjoy discovering the mysteries of life. Bibi Fatuma was still looking at the chest. There were two pull drawers at the front. All chests normally had a secret hidden compartment deep inside. She lifted the wood that was the base of the chest and it came off. She stared at the chest, then looked up at the boys and smiled. Her eyes sparkled. She put her hand in the deep compartment and took out a sisal bag that was tied with a rope on the neck. The sisal bag looked similar to what the boys had found in the clock. She put the box down and tried to untie the knot of the rope, it was very tight. Baba reached for the toolbox and took out a big pair of scissors. He cut off the rope and Bibi Fatuma gently turned over the bag to empty the contents. Rubies the size of cherries and lemons rolled out! There were smaller stones coloured green and white. "Oh my God! Diamonds and emeralds!" Bibi Fatuma whispered. She opened the drawers in front of the chest and both had sisal bags. She emptied those out on her palms; both the bags had smaller stones; emeralds, rubies, diamonds, sapphires, and pearls!

The boys looked at each other. They jumped to their feet and did a twirl! "We are the Detectives of Shangani!" they sang. Mzee Kasuku added to their tune by adding a chorus, "Detectives did it! Detectives did it! Detectives did it!"

Then Bakari turned to Bibi Fatuma and held out the ruby that he had carried in his pocket and gave it to her. It was the one that Bibi Fatuma had told him to throw in the ocean. Bibi Fatuma smiled. "I'll take all those Bibi Fatuma to throw in the middle of the ocean if you like," he winked at her as he said that. Bibi Fatuma chuckled, "I appreciate that Bakari, but I don't think there will be a need for that." Bakari was glad that Bibi Fatuma realised her mistake and no longer believed that stones could bring good or bad fortune. That was in God's hands alone.

Epilogue

Bakari, Omari, and Mzee Kasuku treated themselves to a day at the beach after all their hard detective work. They passed by Mr. Barretto's shop to buy some crisps, water, and soft drinks. "Aha, the Detectives of Shangani, you have a story to tell me I believe," said Mr. Barretto. He gave them a soda each as they narrated the story to him in a summarised version. Mr. Barretto listened attentively making some sounds of amazement in between. "I will give you an award for solving a mystery!" He said winking and giving them each a packet of crisps. The boys thanked him and made their way towards the beach.

"Oh, this is the life," Bakari said as he stretched himself on the sand. "I just love the beach," Omari added. "Life is the beach, the beach is the life," Mzee Kasuku said, combining the boys' sentences. Their school vacation had turned out to be extraordinary. They had solved a mystery, found hidden rubies, saved Bibi Fatuma from a crook, and now they were relaxing on the beach. Just then, Omari nudged Bakari. "What is it? Let me soak in more of the sun," he replied lazily with his eyes shut. "Bakari! Bakari! Look!" Omari nearly shouted. He heard the urgency in Omari's tone and quickly sat up. "What is it?" he asked irritably. "Look." Omari said pointing towards the sea. It looked like someone's arm had been chopped off and washed ashore! They ran down towards the waves. On closer inspection the boys realised it was a wooden arm. "I wonder who this wooden arm belongs to," Omari said. The boys looked at each other. Bakari's eyes twinkled and he smiled. "It looks like we may have another mystery to solve!" Bakari exclaimed. "Watch out! The Detectives of Shangani are here!" Mzee Kasuku shouted.

Glossary

Adhaan	call to prayer
Attire	to dress, especially in fine or formal clothes
Baba	father
Bajia	deep-fried small balls of cooked mashed potato/yams
Bewilderment	is a state of being confused and puzzled
Bibi	grandmother
Big-G	a brand of chewing gum
Biriyani	an Indian dish containing rice with meat or vegetables, cooked in spices
Calligraphy	decorative handwriting or handwritten lettering.
Changu	type of fish
Dada	sister
Daladala	town/city commuter bus (common in cities of Tanzania)
Darajani	market place in Zanzibar town in an alleyway with dozens of small shops selling everything from perfume to electronics

Forodhani	Forodhani Gardens are located facing the Indian Ocean. Locals are attracted to this garden as there are many food vendors. It also faces the House of Wonders
Habari yako?	how are you?
Inscription	engraving
Instinct	a powerful motivation or impulse.
Interrogate	ask questions of (someone) closely or formally.
Jambiani	Jambiani is a village with about 8000 inhabitants. It is located at the south-eastern part of Zanzibar, 40 kilometres from the capital Stone Town
Jinn	a class of spirits belived to be capable of appearing in human and animal forms and influencing humankind for either good or evil
Kahawa	coffee
Kanzu	a long usually white garment worn by men in Africa
Karibu	welcome
Khanga	a traditional garment with colourful patterns and a proverb written on the base of it. It is worn by the people of East Africa
Kofia	a round shaped head covering with a flat top and adorned with designs all over

Kwaheri	goodbye
Maandazi	(pl): Andazi (s) Made from white wheat flour, water, coconut cream (or margarine), sugar and yeast. The dough which is similar to that of doughnut, is rolled out on a board, cut into diamond shapes or rounds and allowed to rise for one or two hours. The maandazi are then deep fried to golden color. Can be served with red beans or curries and also can be served with tea.
Madrassah	a place where children learn religious studies
Maghreb	evening prayer
Magnificent	extremely beautiful, elaborate, or impressive.
Masjid	a place of prayer for Muslims
Mishkaki	meat cut into small pieces and barbequed on a skewer
Paan	an Indian tradition of chewing betel leaf (Piper betle) with areca nut and slaked lime paste
Possession	the state of having, owning, or controlling something.
Optimistic	hopeful and confident about the future.

Salama	A word used to greet people and means is everything okay
Shokishoki	Rambutan (type of fruit)
Spacious	having ample space.
Sparkling	shining brightly with flashes of light.
Stammer	say something with difficulty, repeating the initial letters of words and with sudden involuntary pauses.
Syndicate	a group of individuals or organizations combined to promote a common interest.
Tree house	a structure built in the branches of a tree for children to play in.
Vitumbua:	(pl) Kitumbua (s)sweet biting made of rice flour, coconut milk, sugar and yeast. Very popular for breakfast
Zuhr	afternoon prayer